18/06/21

16/08/21

Sou

KT-215-727

WITHDRAWN

WITHDRAWN

Books should be returned or renewed by the last date above. Renew by phone **03000 41 31 31** or online *www.kent.gov.uk/libs*

C334086554

A Year of
Beautiful Eating

MADELEINE SHAW

A Year of
Beautiful Eating

Eat fresh. Eat seasonal. Glow with health, all year round.

MADELEINE SHAW

TRAPEZE

Contents

Introduction

Hello and welcome to *A Year of Beautiful Eating*! As a kid at school, I never knew what I wanted to do. I didn't particularly excel at anything (apart from smiling), but when I started to work in food and wellness something changed in me. I knew then that I wanted to dedicate myself to making healthy eating a part of everyone's life – and making it something fun, delicious and easy to adopt. This book is all about keeping it simple. No food fads, just getting back to good produce in tune with nature. The way we used to eat.

I wasn't always healthy before I got into cooking. I had been in a total food rut, existing on low-fat yogurt, Diet Coke, granola, rice cakes and the odd bit of dried fruit. That was it: no variety, just bland, boring and joyless food. Not only that, what I ate was packed full of hidden sugars! Without realising it, I was pretty much living on the stuff – and all in the name of being on a 'healthy' diet.

When I moved to Australia and discovered my passion for food, I had to unlearn all my bad habits. A key step was understanding that something calling itself 'low fat' was probably high in refined sugars and would be much, much worse for me than a full-fat option. Gradually, I went from eating a low-fat, restrictive diet to something I would never call a diet – it was a way of eating that nourished me from the inside out, full of fresh ingredients, wholefoods and healthy fats. These foods kept me feeling sustained throughout the day. The negative thoughts about diet and deprivation were banished and I became excited about the different ways I could heap goodness on to my plate and into my body.

I became passionate about sharing my knowledge with others, fascinated by flavour combinations and by the medicinal properties our food can possess. My training, first as a nutritional health coach and later as a nutritional therapist, really helped me to understand exactly which delicious nutrients make our skin glow, our hair shine and our eyes sparkle.

Understanding the nutrients foods contain goes hand-in-hand with seasonality. I first started thinking about eating in tune with nature when I happened to eat a strawberry in winter one day; it was watery, tasteless and expensive because it had been grown on the other side of the world and ripened in transit. My mind flashed back to strawberry picking as a little girl and the delight I would experience from finding plump, sun-ripened fruit on the plant. There was nothing delightful about that poor, grey, winter strawberry I had eaten. I vowed that day that I would stick to eating berries in the summer (unless frozen) and I started to shop in my local farmers' market, seeking out what was in season.

But seasonal food isn't just about taste: it's kinder on your bank balance and on the environment too. Plus, it's what your body wants at that moment in time. In the winter, root veggies thrive and we really need their starchy deliciousness — cooked up in warming soups — because our bodies are using up much more energy in the cold. Conversely, when the days grow longer and the summer's heat is at its beautiful peak, the abundance of cooling foods like lettuces, cucumbers and courgettes should be taken advantage of.

This book will take you on a year-long journey through the food of the seasons: I'll show you how to boost your vitamin D levels in winter, how to protect your precious skin in the summer months with SPF-rich smoothies, and how healthy fats can be a real remedy for dry skin, whatever the season. To help you on your way, keep an eye out for these symbols so you can choose, at a glance, which recipes you'd like to cook:

Vegan	V	Vitamin D rich	D
Vegetarian	V	Protein packed	PP
Gluten free	GF	Under 15 mins	15
Dairy free	DF	Under 30 mins	30
Good for skin	S		

I hope this book gives you the tools to understand what your food should be doing for you — and helps you to maximise that beautiful glow, from the inside out, whatever the weather.

Enjoy eating yourself beautiful!

Madeleine x

Reasons to Go Seasonal and Local

There's nothing better than the freshness of asparagus on a crisp spring evening, or the sweetness of a juicy strawberry in summer. Earthy beetroot in autumn and the rich velvetiness of celeriac in winter make for the perfect supper. There are so many reasons why eating seasonally is good for you, but if you still need convincing, read on!

Taste

There is a huge movement in restaurant kitchens for chefs to source more of their ingredients locally, which also means seasonally – and that's because they know it's the best way to guarantee great taste. So let's follow suit in our kitchens at home.

As with the strawberries from my childhood, fresh produce equals easy cooking as it's already bursting with flavour. Seasonal, locally sourced fruit and veg is picked when ripe so there is less time for it to lose its flavour and health benefits.

Variety is the Spice of Life

Is it a classic tomato salad or steamed broccoli that's always on your plate on the side? We are creatures of habit and often end up going to the same aisles buying the same veggies every week.

It's amazing how many different fruits and vegetables there are and being more aware of what's in season will help you to step out of your food rut and introduce a bit more delicious variety into your life. I also get a weekly veg box delivered; sometimes vegetables turn up that I have never eaten or cooked with before so it keeps things interesting – and, as I really hate waste, the box delivery makes me focus on eating up all my veggies!

Community Love

When you choose locally grown ingredients you are supporting your community, your nearest town and your country. You boost the local economy and create a social network without even thinking about it.

In New Zealand, many people have access to farms that sell their produce direct to consumers. I'm sure this happens in lots of places around the world, but it definitely doesn't happen down my road so I really try and make an effort to shop locally.

There is something heart-warming about buying meat from my local butcher or veggies from a local farmers' market. That butcher or stallholder has passion for the food they are selling and can often offer great tips for how and what to cook with it. Their advice makes me feel connected to the farm as well as to the ingredients I am buying. Alternatively, you can still keep it local if you're shopping at a supermarket; just read the label and have a think about where the produce is from.

Cost

Food bills can add up – especially when you are buying lots of fresh produce – but seasonal choices keep costs down. When you buy in season you are buying fruit and veg at their peak, in taste AND supply. Larger quantities lead to more efficient processes so it costs the farmers and distributors less to get produce to you, and this discount is passed on in the price.

My Tips for Eating in Tune with Nature

You can start cooking from this book at any point in the year. There are enough recipes to get you through each season – by the time you've finished one section, the next season will be around the corner to tempt you with a whole new array of treats. To help you on your way, here are some tips to make eating in tune with nature easy-peasy!

The right equipment

With the right kitchen gadgets, you can whip up all kinds of wonders in minutes. These are the three main tools I use when cooking:

Food processor – good for making raw desserts, cauliflower rice and cakes

Blender – perfect for smoothies and soups

Spiraliser – essential for making noodles from veggies such as carrots and courgettes

Stock up your pantry

There are some staples that I always stock up on for my store cupboard as they are used in the majority of my recipes. Buy a few of these items every time you do your food shop, and you'll soon have a cupboard bursting with health-boosting goodies.

Flours: spelt flour, buckwheat flour

Oils and vinegars: coconut oil, butter, extra virgin olive oil, avocado oil, apple cider vinegar

Grains: quinoa, wild rice, buckwheat, oats

Nuts and seeds: flaked almonds, almond milk, almond butter, peanut butter, pumpkin seeds

Spices and seasoning: turmeric, ground cinnamon, cumin, smoked paprika, sea salt, peppercorns to grind, chilli flakes, mustard, tamari, fresh ginger, garlic

Sweeteners: coconut sugar, honey, maple syrup

Bread: rye bread, sourdough

Pulses and legumes: lentils, chickpeas, black beans

Buy in bulk

My favourite section of the supermarket is world foods, where you can find big kilogram bags of brown rice, and cheap dates and nuts. Not many people know about this; they head straight for aisles with the big brand names, but end up paying twice the price. The world food aisle is now my first port of call – make sure you swing by next time, and see for yourself!

Go to specialist shops

If your local supermarket isn't big on world foods then hit up specialist shops. If you like making raw desserts then dates are a key ingredient. I love going to my local Middle Eastern shop, which stocks fresh dates that are by far the juiciest and tastiest I have ever found in London.

Eat less expensive cuts of meat

Chicken breasts and prime beef steaks are easy to cook but can be the most expensive cuts of meat. Try a shoulder or a shank instead, use stewing steak or chicken thighs. These are cheaper and taste delicious when slow-cooked.

Plan and prep

You don't end up with lots of wasted food when you plan your meals. There is nothing worse than old, limp spinach in the fridge, not to mention all the money that costs. Take out your notepad and get planning.

Revamp leftovers

Don't throw out those leftovers – revamp them! Leftover roast chicken is great shredded in an avocado sandwich or salad. Heat that stew up again and serve it with some fresh tomato salsa and corn chips. Cooked veggies come to life sautéed in a stir-fry with chilli and garlic, blended into soups or thrown in a pan with some eggs to make a frittata.

Stop buying snacks

Shop-bought snacks can be expensive, full of refined sugars and rarely hit the hunger spot. Stick to eating bigger portions at meals or try some of my home-made snack ideas.

Top Ten Foods for Glowing Skin and When to Eat Them

I spend most of my time online, writing pieces for my blog and chatting with my readers. One of the most common questions I get asked is: 'What foods can I eat to help my skin?' You can buy the most expensive creams in the world, but if you're not eating right it will show up in your skin. All foods have their own nutritional qualities, but some trump the rest when it comes to skin-glowing benefits. Here is a list of my top ten.

1. Salmon

Season: Late winter, spring and summer

Benefits: I love salmon! Not only does it taste delicious every way you cook it, but salmon is also a nutritional powerhouse. It's packed full of omega 3 fatty acids (these strengthen the skin's cell membranes, allowing nutrients to pass through, and act as anti-inflammatories), magnesium, selenium and all the B vitamins. Selenium is an amazing antioxidant and helps to reduce skin ageing and acne.

How to eat: In the summer, marinate a salmon steak in some chilli and garlic then BBQ it. Salmon is also lovely when poached with new potatoes in spring. Eat the smoked variety on rye bread for a late winter breakfast.

Recipes with salmon: pages 20, 40 and 62

2. Kale

Season: Autumn, winter and early spring

Benefits: Of all the super-healthy leafy greens, kale is king. It's loaded with vitamins, minerals, fibre, antioxidants and various bioactive compounds. Kale contains vitamin C, vitamin A and vitamin K1. We all know vitamin C is good for colds, but it also helps fade skin pigmentation and stops inflammation in its tracks.

How to eat: Rub the leaves in oil and roast them as chips. Sauté chopped kale and team with a juicy steak. Alternatively use the full leaves as wraps.

Recipes with kale: pages 158, 216 and 224

3. Seaweed

Season: Spring and summer (but it can be eaten all year round)

Benefits: There are thousands of different plant species in the ocean, some of which are incredibly nutritious. Seaweed is particularly high in minerals such as calcium, iron, magnesium and manganese. Where seaweed really shines, though, is with its high content of iodine, a mineral that is used to make thyroid hormones (which regulate your metabolism). Calcium is a skin saver, as it increases cell renewal, lipid-barrier function and antioxidant protection.

How to eat: Steam first then either add to an Asian stir-fry, team with some sashimi to make your nori rolls or sprinkle into a miso salad.

Recipes with seaweed: There aren't any in this book, but sprinkle it on salads, add to Asian soups and ask for a seaweed salad at Japanese restaurants.

4. Garlic

Season: Summer and autumn

Benefits: Garlic is high in vitamins C, B1, B6 and minerals like calcium, potassium, copper, manganese and selenium. It is also loaded with antibacterial and antifungal properties that help unblock pores and reduce breakouts.

How to eat: Peel and crush into stir-fries, roast whole with your Sunday roast or add chopped raw garlic to dressings.

Recipes with garlic: There are lots to choose from. My favourites are pages 24, 102 and 187.

5. Shellfish

Season: Different varieties are available all year round

Benefits: Clams are amongst the best sources of vitamin B12 in existence, with 100g of clams supplying over sixteen times the recommended daily amount. Vitamin B12 is essential for beautiful skin as it is key in repairing skin cells. Clams are also loaded with lots of other vitamins and minerals, including vitamin C, other B vitamins, potassium, selenium and iron.

How to eat: Whip up a garlic and white wine sauce and steam your mussels or clams in it. Or pan-fry some prawns with garlic and chilli.

Recipes with shellfish: pages 48, 62 and 187

6. Oysters

Season: Autumn and winter

Benefits: Extravagant but incredibly nutritious: 100g of oysters supply six times the recommended daily amount (RDA) of zinc, twice the RDA of copper, along with large amounts of vitamins B12 and D. Zinc has been linked to helping clear up acne and repairing damaged tissue.

How to eat: Treat yourself to some freshly shucked oysters (carefully cut from their shell). They are served on a bed of crushed ice and eaten raw. I love them with lemon juice but you can also add some vinegar and red onion for a bit more kick.

Recipes with oysters: Sadly there are none. Save eating them for when you're by the seaside, washed down with a glass of wine!

7. Blueberries

Season: Summer

Benefits: Blueberries stand out in the fruit department. They are loaded with powerful antioxidant substances, including anthocyanins and several phytochemicals, which protect the skin from sun and pollution damage.

How to eat: Add fresh blueberries to muffins and porridge, snack on them or whizz them up in your favorite smoothie.

Recipes with blueberries: pages 83, 130 and 140

8. Eggs

Season: All year round

Benefits: Whole eggs are so nutritious that they're often referred to as nature's multivitamin. Eggs contain collagen, which is a time-trusted skin anti-ageing ingredient.

How to eat: Pop a fried egg on top of a roasted corn salad, or scramble your eggs with chopped coriander and chilli then serve with sourdough toast. It's up to you – they go with everything.

Recipes with eggs: pages 88, 156 and 209

9. Raw Cacao

Season: All year round

Benefits: Raw cacao is loaded with fibre, iron, magnesium, copper and manganese. It also contains an amazing range of antioxidants, which protect the skin from sun damage.

How to eat: Add to smoothies to get that chocolate fix, put a pinch into your bolognese to bring out the flavour and dust it over desserts for a rich finish.

Recipes with raw cacao: pages 28, 135 and 254

10. Turmeric

Season: All year round

Benefits: Turmeric contains compounds called curcuminoids, which have powerful anti-inflammatory effects and are very strong antioxidants.

How to eat: For a delicious drink, add turmeric, ginger and cardamom to almond milk. Turmeric gives that rich colour to Indian curries, or you can mix it with chicken mince to spice up your chicken burgers.

Recipes with turmeric: pages 47, 177 and 235

What's in Season?

Spring

Fruit: bananas, blood oranges, kiwi fruit, lemons, oranges, passion fruit, pineapple, rhubarb

Veg: asparagus, broccoli, carrots, cauliflower, Jersey Royal new potatoes, kale, leeks, lettuce and salad leaves, peas, purple sprouting broccoli, radishes, rocket, samphire, spinach, spring onions, watercress, wild nettles

Meat and Poultry: lamb, wood pigeon

Fish and Shellfish: cockles, Dover sole, hake, langoustine, lemon sole, lobster, mussels, red mullet, salmon, shrimps, whitebait

Summer

Fruit: apricots, bilberries, blueberries, cherries, damsons, figs, greengages, loganberries, melons, nectarines, peaches, plums, raspberries, redcurrants, strawberries

Veg: artichoke, aubergine, beetroot, broad beans, broccoli, carrots, chillies, courgettes, cucumber, fennel, French beans, garlic, Jersey Royal new potatoes, kohlrabi, lettuce and salad leaves, mangetout, onions, pak choi, peas, radishes, rocket, runner beans, samphire, spinach, spring onions, tomatoes, turnips, watercress, wild nettles

Meat and Poultry: lamb, rabbit, wood pigeon

Fish and Shellfish: cod, coley, crab, Dover sole, haddock, halibut, herring, langoustine, mackerel, plaice, pollack, prawns, salmon, sardines, scallops (queen), sea bass (wild), sea bream, sea trout, shrimps, squid, whelks, whitebait

Autumn

Fruit: apples, bilberries, blackberries, damsons, elderberries, figs, grapes, medlars, melons, nectarines, peaches, pears, plums, raspberries, redcurrants

Veg: artichoke, aubergine, beetroot, broccoli, butternut squash, carrots, celeriac, celery, chillies, courgettes, cucumber, fennel, French beans, garlic, horseradish, kale, kohlrabi, leeks, lettuce and salad leaves, mangetout, marrow, onions, parsnips, pak choi, peppers, potatoes (main crop), pumpkin, radishes, rocket, runner beans, shallots, spring onions, sweetcorn, tomatoes, turnips, watercress, wild mushrooms

Meat and Poultry: beef, duck, goose, grouse, guinea fowl, hare, lamb, mallard, partridge, pheasant, rabbit, turkey, venison, wood pigeon

Fish and Shellfish: clams, cod, coley, crab, dab, Dover sole, grey mullet, gurnard, haddock, halibut, hake, herring, lemon sole, lobster, mackerel, monkfish, mussels, oysters, pilchard, plaice, pollock, prawns, red mullet, sea bass (wild), sea bream, skate, squid, turbot, winkles

Winter

Fruit: apples, blood oranges, clementines, cranberries, passion fruit, pears, pineapple, pomegranate, satsumas, tangerines

Veg: beetroot, Brussels sprouts, cauliflower, celeriac, celery, chicory, horseradish, Jerusalem artichoke, kale, kohlrabi, leeks, parsnips, potatoes (main crop), salsify, shallots, swede, truffles (black), truffles (white), turnips, wild mushrooms

Meat and Poultry: duck, goose, grouse, guinea fowl, hare, mallard, partridge, pheasant, rabbit, turkey, venison

Fish and Shellfish: clams, cod, coley, dab, Dover sole, gurnard, haddock, halibut, hake, langoustine, lemon sole, lobster, mackerel, monkfish, mussels, oysters, plaice, red mullet, salmon, scallops (queen), sea bass (wild), sea bream, skate, turbot, winkles

Spring

Breakfast

Glowing Breakfast Muffins

Quinoa and Chia Bread

Four Spring Ways on Toast: Avocado with Maple Miso Dressing and Pomegranate, Lemon and Pea Pesto Smash, Chargrilled Asparagus and Chimichurri, Rhubarb and Pistachios

Chocolate Protein Powered Smoothie

Spring-in-Your-Step Juice

Zesty Ricotta Pancakes

Soups, Salads and Snacks

Four Spring Side Salads: Shaved Fennel and Rocket Salad, Grilled Asparagus, Burrata and Artichoke Salad, Leeks and Romesco, Asian Sprouting Broccoli with Toasted Sesame Seeds and Miso Dressing

Roasted Cauliflower with Romesco, Capers and Toasted Hazelnuts

Oregano-Infused Potato Salad with Fennel and Leeks

Avocado, Radish and Salmon Boats

Whole Roasted Cauliflower with Yogurt Dressing

Greek Goodness Salad

Mixed Veggie Soup

Two Spring Lunch Boxes: Prawn, Grapefruit and Avocado Salad, Buckwheat Tabbouleh with Rocket, Radishes and Spring Onion

Two Spring Take-to-Work Snacks: Roasted Chickpeas, Rice Crispy Squares

Mains

Tray-Roasted Cod with Olives, Smoked Paprika and Asparagus

Beef Kebabs with Mint Raita

Grilled Herb-Crusted Mackerel

Tray-Baked Chicken with Tomato and Fennel

Spanish Chickpea Stew with Chorizo and Spinach

Fish Skewers with Parsnips Chips

Maple and Miso Red Rice Salad

Lamb Chops with Parsnip Mash and Asparagus

Dessert

Rhubarb and Coconut Rice Pudding

Raw Coconut and Chocolate Bars

Choc Chip and Raisin Blondie Brownies

Coffee Pecan Muffins

Glowing Breakfast Muffins

GF DF S D PP 30

These are my favourite take-to-work breakfast muffins. The saltiness of the sun-dried tomatoes goes so well with the crunch of the spring onions and the freshly chopped dill. These egg muffins can be made the night before for the perfect on-the-go brekkie. They're quick, easy and fit perfectly in my Tupperware. You can eat them on their own for brekkie or combine with a salad for your lunch.

Makes 6 muffins, serves 3

3 spring onions
4 sun-dried tomatoes
50g smoked salmon
6 eggs
salt and freshly ground
   black pepper, to taste
1 tbsp chopped fresh dill
coconut oil, for greasing

Preheat the oven to 200°C/400°F/gas mark 6.

Finely chop the spring onions and slice up the sun-dried tomatoes. Cut the smoked salmon into small pieces. Beat the eggs in a bowl with some freshly ground pepper and a pinch of salt. Add the chopped spring onions, sun-dried tomatoes, smoked salmon and dill. Mix well. Grease a six-hole muffin tin with coconut oil, then spoon the mixture into the tin.

Bake in the oven for 15 minutes, until golden on top. Eat hot, or cool on a rack to pack up and bring into work.

These muffins will last for 3 days in the fridge.

Quinoa and Chia Bread

V GF DF S PP

I learnt to make this bread on a retreat in Ibiza. The chef, Ben, was so generous he would give me extra rations of quinoa bread with almond butter and banana when I was hungry and I became addicted to it. So simple and tasty. Gluten-free breads can often be awful and full of rubbish, but this one is a total winner.

Makes 1 loaf

300g quinoa
75g chia seeds
125ml water
50g avocado oil or
    melted coconut oil, plus
    extra for greasing
½ tsp gluten-free
    bicarbonate of soda
½ tsp salt
¼ tsp ground black pepper
2 tbsp lemon juice
100g pumpkin seeds
1 tsp dried garlic powder
2 tbsp poppy seeds
2 tbsp chopped fresh
    rosemary
2 tbsp chopped fresh
    thyme

The night before you make this, place the quinoa in a bowl and cover it in just-boiled water, then leave to soak. This will slightly cook the quinoa, making it easier to blend and more digestible.

Put the chia seeds into a bowl and add the cold water, then leave to soak overnight too, so it forms into a gel.

The next day, preheat the oven to 170°C/325°F/gas mark 3.

Drain the quinoa well in a sieve, letting it drip for 15 minutes so it's totally dry. Blend for 30 seconds in a food processor, then add the rest of the ingredients. Blend for a few more minutes until fully combined.

Grease a loaf tin with plenty of oil and pour in the mixture. Bake for 1 hour and 20 minutes until cooked through. Allow to completely cool in the tin, then remove and slice into 2cm slices and toast.

This goes so well with smashed avocado, almond butter or dipped into soups or runny eggs.

This loaf will last for 2 weeks in the fridge but you can also freeze it for up to 2 months.

Four Spring Ways on Toast

Toast is a staple – it's probably the way you start the day. But why not whack on some seasonal veggies and a bit of spice? This will make breakfast a totally new and awesome experience. Toast two slices of rye, sourdough or gluten-free bread and pile on the topping of your choice.

Serves 2

1 large avocado
seeds from ¼ pomegranate

For the maple miso dressing

2 tbsp almond butter
2 tbsp sweet white miso
3 tbsp brown rice vinegar
1 tbsp lemon juice
2 tbsp toasted sesame oil
1 tbsp maple syrup
pinch of cayenne pepper
pinch of salt, to taste
2–4 tbsp water

Avocado

(V) GF DF (S) 15

with Maple Miso Dressing and Pomegranate

Mix together all the maple miso dressing ingredients in a jug, adding the water last, a tablespoon at a time, until you get a good pouring consistency. Cut the avocado in half, peel and stone it, and mash the flesh with a fork. Spread the avocado evenly on to your toast and pour half a tablespoon of the dressing over each slice. Top with the pomegranate seeds and enjoy.

This maple miso dressing lasts for a week in the fridge and is perfect on all sorts of salads.

Serves 2

200g frozen peas
1 small garlic clove, crushed
grated zest and juice of ½ lemon
2 tbsp almond butter
50g fresh basil
big pinch of salt
50ml olive oil
2 tbsp toasted sunflower seeds
1 tsp tamari

Lemon and Pea Pesto Smash

(V) GF DF (S) 15

Blend the peas, garlic, lemon juice, almond butter, basil, 1 teaspoon of the lemon zest, the salt and the olive oil together. Pile this pesto smash on your toast, then top with the toasted seeds and tamari

Serves 2

½ small bunch of
  asparagus
1 tbsp coconut oil or
  butter

For the chimichurri

25g fresh coriander,
  finely chopped
25g fresh parsley,
finely chopped
1 jalapeño chilli, deseeded
  and finely chopped
60ml olive oil
1 tbsp red wine vinegar
pinch of salt

Chargrilled Asparagus and Chimichurri

V GF DF 15

Cut the ends off the asparagus and slice in half lengthways. Heat a griddle pan to a high heat, add the oil and let it melt, then place the asparagus in the pan. Griddle for 3–4 minutes until cooked through, turning the asparagus every minute. Meanwhile combine the chimichurri ingredients together in a bowl. Top your toast with the griddled asparagus and spoon over the chimichurri.

This chimichurri dressing will keep for 5 days in the fridge. It jazzes up any salad and goes really well with meat and fish.

Serves 2

6 tbsp rhubarb compote,
  warmed (see page 68)
2 tbsp chopped pistachios

Rhubarb and Pistachios

V GF DF S PP 15

Smear the rhubarb compote on to your toast and top with the pistachios. Halve the quantities for a quick afternoon snack for one.

Serves 1

handful of spinach,
  washed

1 tbsp raw cacao powder

1 frozen banana

1 tbsp almond butter
  or other nut butter

1 tsp vanilla extract

2 tbsp raw vegan
  protein powder

300ml rice milk

pinch of ground
  cinnamon

1 tbsp chia seeds

2 ice cubes

Chocolate Protein Powered Smoothie

I love this smoothie, it's my favourite smoothie to have after a workout. Kieran and I usually make his and hers versions, but this recipe is one we both love and it fills us right up until lunchtime. It's especially good for when we start to see a bit more sun, because raw cacao is bursting with polyphenols and catechins – antioxidants that protect our skin from sunburn and skin cancer. An excuse to eat more raw chocolate?! I'm in . . .

Place everything in a blender and blend until smooth.

Serves 1

1 fennel bulb

2 apples, cored

50g spinach, washed

handful of watercress,
  washed

knob of fresh ginger,
  peeled

juice of 1 lemon

Spring-in-Your-Step Juice

V GF DF S I5

Fennel adds an amazing aromatic element to a juice. Blended with spinach, watercress and lemon – some of the most skin-glowing nutrients – it will make you feel like a Hollywood star.

Roughly chop up the veg and fruit. Put through a juicer and stir in the lemon juice, then serve immediately.

Please note: this is a juice, not a smoothie, so it should be made in a juicer, not a blender.

This juice will last for I day in the fridge.

Zesty Ricotta Pancakes

V S PP 15

We all love pancakes but when I first made these I jumped for joy! Fresh, light, sweet and creamy all at the same time. Ricotta pancakes are always found on the best brunch menus in Australia. Drizzled with maple syrup and crunchy pistachios, this brekkie will make you jump out of bed in no time.

Makes 8 pancakes, serves 2

2 eggs, separated

2 tbsp coconut sugar

grated zest of 1 lemon

60g ricotta cheese, drained

3 tbsp almond milk or other milk

1 tsp vanilla extract

65g spelt flour or gluten-free flour

pinch of salt

3 tbsp coconut oil

maple syrup, to serve

chopped pistachios, to serve

freeze-dried raspberries, to serve

In a large bowl beat the egg yolks, sugar and lemon zest together for a minute. Make sure all the water has been drained from the ricotta, then add to the mixture. Pour in the milk and vanilla, and stir together. Sift in the flour and salt and stir well. In another bowl beat the egg whites until they form stiff peaks. Very carefully, fold the beaten egg whites into the mixture a little at a time.

Heat 1 tablespoon of the coconut oil in a large pan on a medium heat. Pour 2 tablespoons of the mixture into the pan and cook the pancake for 2–3 minutes until golden. Then flip over and cook for another 2 minutes on the other side. Repeat with the rest of the mixture, adding a little more coconut oil to the pan between pancakes when necessary.

Plate up your pancakes and drizzle with maple syrup, sprinkling over some chopped pistachios and freeze-dried raspberries.

Four Spring Side Salads

Serves 4

1 fennel bulb
50g rocket
30g flaked almonds

For the dressing

1 tbsp apple cider vinegar
2 tbsp olive oil
2 tbsp lemon juice
2 tbsp chopped fresh dill
pinch of salt

Shaved Fennel and Rocket Salad   V GF DF S 15

Fennel is so crunchy and perfect for a spring day. This salad helps stimulate your digestive system thanks to the fiery rocket and apple cider vinegar. It's fresh and light and will outshine your main dish!

Mix the dressing ingredients together. Thinly slice the fennel into slivers, then toss with the rocket and almonds. Pour over the dressing.

Serves 2

bunch of asparagus
1 tbsp olive oil
salt, to taste
100g burrata or
    mozzarella
4 olive-oil-marinated
    artichokes, drained
    and quartered
grated zest and juice
    of 1 lemon
1 tbsp chopped fresh
    parsley

Grilled Asparagus, Burrata and Artichoke Salad   V GF D 15

When asparagus comes into season you have to make the most of it. Teamed with creamy burrata, it's a match made in heaven.

Cut the ends off the asparagus and slice in half lengthways, then quarter. Heat a griddle pan to a high heat, pour in the oil and add the asparagus with a pinch of salt. Grill for a few minutes on each side until cooked through. Rip the burrata or mozzarella into bite-sized chunks and mix with the griddled asparagus and the artichokes in a bowl. Pour over the juice from half the lemon, sprinkle over all the lemon zest, a little salt and the parsley, then serve.

Leeks and Romesco

Serves 4

4 leeks, trimmed

salt and freshly ground
   black pepper, to taste

1 bay leaf

1 tbsp chopped fresh
   rosemary

2 garlic cloves, sliced

2 tbsp avocado oil
   or melted butter

200ml veggie or
   chicken stock

4 tbsp Romesco sauce
   (see page 36)

You don't often see roasted leeks on the menu but once you've made this dish it will become a regular on your table in no time. Topped with my magical romesco sauce, it's pure heaven on a plate.

Preheat the oven to 200°C/400°F/gas mark 6. Cut the leeks in half then quarters lengthways. Place in a roasting tray with a pinch of salt and grind of pepper, the bay leaf, rosemary and garlic. Drizzle over the oil and cover with the stock. Roast for 50 minutes until cooked through. Serve the leeks with the Romesco sauce on top.

Asian Sprouting Broccoli
with Toasted Sesame Seeds and Miso Dressing

Serves 4

2 tbsp sesame seeds

200g sprouting broccoli

For the miso dressing

2 tbsp miso paste

1 tbsp maple syrup

1 tbsp sesame oil

2 tbsp rice wine vinegar

2 tbsp lemon juice

3 tbsp olive oil

salt and freshly ground
   black pepper, to taste

Broccoli can be a bit boring on it's own, but when you add this miso dressing it transforms it into the best side dish!

Heat a small frying pan to a medium–high heat and toast the sesame seeds for a minute or two until golden, shaking the pan to prevent them burning. Transfer to a plate and leave to cool. Steam the broccoli over a pan of simmering water for 4 minutes until just cooked through, then drain. Whisk the dressing ingredients together and pour over the broccoli. Top with the toasted sesame seeds.

This salad will last for 2 days in the fridge but is best served hot.

Roasted Cauliflower

V GF DF S

with Romesco, Capers and Toasted Hazelnuts

I'm obsessed with cauliflower, which is why I love spring when cauliflowers are blooming and begging to be roasted. In this recipe I've tossed the florets with salty olives and capers, and sprinkled it with crunchy nuts and peppery rocket. You will be inspired by how quick and easy it is to make such a flavoursome vegetable dish.

Serves 2

1 red onion

1 large cauliflower,
    leaves removed

2 tbsp avocado oil

salt and freshly ground
    black pepper, to taste

sprig of fresh oregano,
    leaves picked and
    chopped

3 tbsp capers

100g Kalamata olives

50g watercress

50g rocket

20g toasted hazelnuts,
    chopped

For the Romesco sauce

juice of 1 lime

80ml olive oil

1 red chilli

4 roasted red peppers
    in olive oil from a jar

20g toasted hazelnuts,
    roughly chopped

2 spring onions,
    roughly chopped

1 garlic clove

¾ tsp salt

Preheat the oven to 180°C/350°F/gas mark 4.

Finely slice the red onion into slivers and chop the cauliflower into small chunks. Put both into a roasting tin and coat in the oil, with a pinch of salt, pepper and the oregano. Add the capers and olives and roast for 30–40 minutes in the oven until golden brown and cooked through.

Meanwhile make the Romesco. Whizz all the ingredients in a blender until smooth.

Toss the roasted cauliflower mixture with the watercress and rocket. Top with a few tablespoons of the Romesco sauce and the chopped hazelnuts. Stir well and serve.

This dish will last for 2 days in the fridge but is best served immediately. The sauce will last for 5 days: add it to savoury breakfasts or salads and dip crudités into it. It's delish!

Oregano-Infused Potato Salad
with Fennel and Leeks

V GF DF S 30

Potatoes have had a bad rep over the years. Sure, they are a bit carby, but cold potatoes are rather spectacular. You see, cold potatoes contain lots of starch . . . which is amazing for your gut. And a healthy gut means clear skin, so let's get munching on those spuds – yum!

Serves 4

2 leeks, trimmed

1 tbsp avocado oil
  or butter

salt and freshly ground
  black pepper, to taste

400g Jersey Royals

50ml veggie or chicken
  stock, just boiled

sprig of fresh oregano,
  leaves picked and
  chopped

100g rocket

1 fennel bulb

2 spring onions

30g walnuts, roughly
  chopped

2 tbsp chopped
  fresh parsley

1 tbsp olive oil

Finely chop the leeks into thin slivers. Heat the oil in a large pan and sauté the leeks with a pinch of salt and pepper for 20 minutes, until golden and caramelised.

While the leeks are cooking, boil the potatoes in a pot of simmering salted water for 20–25 minutes until tender. Drain them and slice in half, then put back into the same pot you cooked them in. Pour over the hot stock and add the oregano and a pinch of salt. Leave while you prep the rest of the salad.

Place the rocket in a bowl. Thinly slice the fennel with a mandolin into fine ribbons and add to the rocket, then tip in the cooked leeks and potatoes. Finely chop the spring onions and throw them over the salad, along with the nuts, parsley, a big pinch of salt and the olive oil. Toss and serve.

Avocado, Radish and Salmon Boats

GF DF S 15

Sometimes you need a little snack or a canapé for a dinner party, and these are the best. You couldn't think of a more skin-loving mixture. Omega 3-rich salmon teamed with the mighty avocado. Just pop these in your mouth and enjoy the benefits.

Makes 8–10 boats, serves 4 as a starter or canapé

2 salmon fillets

1 garlic clove, crushed

2 tsp freshly grated ginger

1 tbsp tamari

1 tbsp coconut oil

1 little gem lettuce

1 avocado, chopped

3 radishes

1 tbsp toasted sesame seeds

juice of 1 lime

pinch of salt

½ red chilli, deseeded and finely sliced

Rub the salmon with the garlic, ginger and tamari. Heat the coconut oil in a large pan over a medium–high heat, allowing it to melt. Starting skin side down, cook the salmon for 2 minutes on each side, so it is just cooked through.

Meanwhile, start to prep the boats. Separate the leaves of the little gem and put on a serving plate. Add some avocado to each boat. With a mandolin or sharp knife, thinly slice the radishes into slivers and divide evenly between the boats. Break the cooked salmon into small chunks and place on top. Add the sesame seeds and drizzle over some lime juice and the salt. Place a sliver of chilli on each boat and serve.

Whole Roasted Cauliflower
with Yogurt Dressing

V GF DF

If you want to show off a little, this veggie dish is perfect. It looks spectacular on the table. Once cooked, it's like slicing into a delicious savoury cake. Smothered in the tantalising tahini yogurt, this is nothing but a showstopper!

Serves 4

1 medium cauliflower,
    leaves removed
1 tbsp coconut oil
1 red onion, chopped
salt and freshly ground
    black pepper, to taste
2 garlic cloves, crushed
1 tbsp freshly grated ginger
1 green chilli, deseeded
    and chopped
400ml can coconut milk,
    cream and coconut milk
    separated
10g fresh coriander,
    divided into stalks
    and leaves
1 tsp coriander seeds
1 tsp ground cumin
1 tsp garam masala

For the dressing

120g coconut yogurt or
    Greek yogurt
2 tbsp lemon juice
3 tbsp tahini
3 tbsp water
pinch of salt

Preheat the oven to 180°C/350°F/gas mark 4.

Place the cauliflower in a pot of simmering salted water and boil for 10 minutes.

While this is cooking, heat the oil in a large pan and sauté the onion for 7 minutes with a pinch of salt and pepper until golden. Add the garlic, ginger and chilli and stir for a minute, then add the cream from the coconut milk, the fresh coriander stalks, coriander seeds and cumin. Cook for another 2 minutes, then add the garam masala and turn off the heat. Blend until a smooth sauce.

Drain the cauliflower and place in a roasting tin. Tip the sauce over the cauliflower, coating thoroughly and rubbing it in. Roast in the oven for 40 minutes until golden.

To make the dressing, blend the yogurt, lemon juice, tahini and the coriander leaves left from earlier with the water and salt until smooth. Pour the dressing over the roasted cauliflower and serve.

Greek Goodness Salad

(V) (DF)

Sometimes I just fancy a nice mezze salad. No cooking, just throwing some delicious ingredients together. These seedy crackers go so well with mezze – they're tasty, crunchy and packed with nutrients.

Serves 2

4 marinated artichokes
100g cherry tomatoes
50g rocket
3 tbsp hummus
100g feta (optional)
2 roasted red peppers in
   olive oil from a
   jar, sliced
100g Kalamata olives
2 tbsp chopped fresh basil
2 tbsp chopped fresh mint

For the crackers

70g sunflower seeds
50g ground flaxseeds
40g sesame seeds
2 tbsp chia seeds
70g porridge oats
1 tbsp chopped fresh
   rosemary
1 tsp salt
½ tsp black pepper
grated zest of 1 lemon
1 tbsp lemon juice
1 tbsp maple syrup
1 tbsp olive oil
230ml water

For the dressing

4 tbsp olive oil
2 tbsp vinegar
juice of ½ lemon
pinch of salt

Preheat the oven to 170°C/325°F/gas mark 3.

To make the crackers, combine all the ingredients in a bowl and stir well. Leave to soak for half an hour so the chia seeds sweat and absorb the water. Line a large baking tray with baking paper and spread the mixture out on top so it is ½cm thin. Bake in the oven for 30 minutes until golden. Remove from the oven and cut into rectangles, then put back in the oven for another 10 minutes, flipping the cracker rectangles halfway through. Allow them to cool as you make the salad.

Mix the oil, vinegar and lemon juice together with the salt to make the dressing. Halve the artichokes and tomatoes. Split the rocket, hummus, feta (if using), artichokes, peppers, olives and tomatoes between two bowls. Throw over the chopped herbs and the dressing and serve with a handful of crackers.

Keep any leftover crackers in an airtight container for 4–5 days.

Mixed Veggie Soup

V GF DF

This soup is creamy, spicy and oh so nourishing. The golden colour from the root veg and turmeric makes you feel like a king. Topped off with the dill and coriander, this soup is the thing I want more than anything else meeting me at home after a long day.

Serves 4

2 red onions
1 celeriac
300g parsnips
1 fennel bulb
2 tbsp oil
salt, to taste
2 garlic cloves, crushed
2 tsp freshly grated ginger
1 tsp ground cumin
1 tsp ground coriander
½ tsp turmeric
400ml can coconut milk
½ mild red chilli
20g fresh coriander
2 beef tomatoes
500ml veggie or
    chicken stock
juice of 1 lime
2 tbsp chopped fresh dill

Finely chop the red onions into slivers. Peel the celeriac and chop into 2½cm cubes. Do the same with the parsnips and fennel. Put the oil into a large pot and sauté the onions with a pinch of salt for 5 minutes until browned. Add the garlic and ginger and stir well for a minute. Add the cumin, coriander, turmeric and 2 tablespoons of water, and stir well for 1 minute until the spices become fragrant. Throw the chopped veggies in and stir again, adding a big pinch of salt. Pour in the coconut milk, then turn down the heat and simmer with the lid on for 15 minutes.

Finely chop the chilli, snip the ends off the coriander and finely chop the roots, then chop the tomatoes. Add to the veg in the pot and pour over the stock. Stir well and simmer for another 30 minutes. Remove from the heat and blend until smooth. Pour in the lime juice. Finely chop the coriander leaves and add to the pot with the dill. Stir through and serve hot.

Two Spring Lunch Boxes

These fresh lunch boxes are as wonderfully colourful as they are tasty. With lots of luscious crunchy veggies, why not team them together for a super lunch box?

Serves 1

1 little gem lettuce, sliced

½ grapefruit, peeled
  and sliced

150g cooked prawns

½ avocado, pitted,
  peeled and sliced

1 tbsp olive oil

1 tsp freshly grated ginger

juice of ½ lime

½ red chilli, deseeded
  and finely chopped

Prawn, Grapefruit and Avocado Salad   GF DF PP 15

Mix the lettuce, grapefruit, prawns and avocado together in your lunch box. Whisk the oil, ginger, lime and chilli together, and pour on top of your salad. Keep in the fridge until lunchtime.

Serves 1

70g cooked buckwheat

1 tomato, diced

¼ cucumber, diced

50g rocket

4 radishes, sliced

1 spring onion, finely
  chopped

2 tbsp chopped fresh
  coriander

salt and freshly ground
  black pepper, to taste

1 tbsp olive oil

juice of ½ lemon

Buckwheat Tabbouleh   V GF DF 15
with Rocket, Radishes and Spring Onion

Put the buckwheat and veggies together in a lunch container. Sprinkle on the coriander and season with a big pinch of salt and pepper and mix well. Keep in the fridge until lunchtime, then pour over the oil and lemon juice just before eating.

Two Spring Take-to-Work Snacks

Snacking is often where we go wrong, as it can be all too easy to grab that doughnut or biscuit. Healthy snacks are easy to prepare, delicious to eat and packed full of goodness, so you can enjoy them guilt free. Sunday is a great day to prep, just pop these delicious morsels in a container to take to work. The only hard thing is resisting the temptation to eat them all in one go.

Roasted Chickpeas

V GF DF PP

Serves 3

400g can chickpeas, rinsed and drained
2 tbsp coconut oil or butter, melted
½ tsp ground cumin
½ tsp chilli powder
pinch of cayenne pepper
½ tsp salt

Preheat the oven to 200°C/400°F/gas mark 6.

Put the chickpeas in a bowl, pour over the melted oil and mix. Add the spices and salt, and mix well to coat. Tip out on to a baking tray, shake the tray so the chickpeas spread out, and put in the oven. Roast for 35 minutes until golden and crispy. Allow to cool, then place in an airtight container.

These roasted chickpeas will last for a few days.

Rice Crispy Squares

V DF S PP

Makes 16 squares

70g almond butter or peanut butter
170g honey
2 tbsp coconut oil
1 tsp vanilla extract
90g puffed rice

Line a 20 x 20cm cake tin with baking paper. Melt the nut butter, honey and coconut oil in a pan over a low heat, stirring everything well together, then take off the heat. Stir in the vanilla and puffed rice until the rice is fully coated. Pour the mixture into the tin and flatten the top with your spatula. Place in the fridge and leave to set for 30 minutes. Then remove the tin from the fridge and cut into squares.

Tray-Roasted Cod

GF DF 30

with Olives, Smoked Paprika and Asparagus

This was the first recipe I tested from this book. It was a lovely spring day, Kieran and I had just gone to the gym and we wanted dinner pronto. The asparagus soaks up all the beautiful flavours of this dish, teamed perfectly with the melt-in-your-mouth cod. This tray-bake dinner is super healthy and it will be on the table in no time.

Serves 4

1½ tsp sweet smoked paprika

2 garlic cloves, crushed

salt and freshly ground black pepper, to taste

4 x 150g cod fillets

200ml fish or chicken stock

200g pitted green olives

2 tbsp capers

bunch of asparagus, trimmed

3 tbsp avocado oil or melted butter

1 lemon

Preheat the oven to 180°C/350°F/gas mark 4.

Mix the smoked paprika, garlic and a pinch of salt and pepper together and rub the mixture into the cod. Then pour the stock into a large roasting tray and scatter in the olives, capers and asparagus. Nestle the cod fillets amongst the veggies and pour the avocado oil over the fish. Thinly slice the lemon into 1cm slivers and place around the cod fillets. Sprinkle salt over the entire dish and bake for 15–20 minutes, until the asparagus and cod are cooked through. Serve hot.

Beef Kebabs
with Mint Raita

GF S PP

I first made these kebabs for my mum. I love going over to my mum's and cooking up a storm for the family. Packed full of spices and teamed with a beautiful, fresh, crunchy cucumber raita, this dish is quick and something everyone will love.

Serves 3–4

500g beef mince

3 garlic cloves, crushed

1 tbsp freshly grated ginger

1 red chilli, deseeded and finely chopped

2 tsp ground cumin

1 tsp garam masala

¼ tsp ground cinnamon

2 tbsp chopped fresh coriander

2 tbsp pine nuts, roughly chopped

1 tsp salt

2 tbsp avocado oil or melted coconut oil

For the mint raita

1 small Lebanese cucumber or ½ regular cucumber

100g Greek yogurt

2 tbsp chopped fresh mint

1 tbsp lemon juice

pinch of salt

First make the mint raita. Peel the cucumber, then deseed by halving lengthways and scooping out the seeds with a teaspoon. Finely chop it, then mix with the yogurt, mint, lemon juice and salt.

For the kebabs, combine the beef mince with all the ingredients except the oil. Roll the spiced mince between your hands into eight 10cm-long sausages and put a skewer through each. Place in the fridge for an hour to harden up and marinate.

Take out the kebabs and brush with the oil. Heat a griddle pan to a high heat and place the kebabs in the pan. Griddle for 5–7 minutes, turning every minute until cooked through. Serve hot with the mint raita.

Any leftover raita can be stored in the fridge in an airtight container for 2–3 days.

Grilled Herb-Crusted Mackerel

GF DF S D

Mackerel is a miracle fish when it comes to skin. Your skin just can't get enough of it! Covered in fresh herbs and laid on a bed of green goodness, this mackerel makes steamed veg and fish a thing of the past and shows how sexy healthy food can be.

Serves 2

1 tbsp finely chopped
    fresh dill
1 tbsp finely chopped
    fresh mint
2 tbsp freshly grated ginger
grated zest and juice of
    1 lemon
2 garlic cloves, crushed
big pinch of salt
2 x 150g mackerel fillets
2 tbsp olive oil
50g rocket
50g watercress
100g radishes, finely
    chopped

For the dressing

2 tbsp olive oil
2 tsp lemon juice
2 tsp mustard
pinch of salt

Mix the chopped herbs, ginger, lemon zest and juice and garlic in a bowl with the salt to make a marinade. Score the mackerel on the skin side, put in a dish and rub in the marinade. Pop in the fridge and leave for 2 hours if possible to soak up all of those flavours.

Take the fish out of the fridge. Pour the oil into a griddle pan or frying pan over a medium–high heat. Place the mackerel fillets in the pan and cook for 4 minutes on each side, so the fish is cooked through.

Whisk the dressing ingredients together. Place the rocket, watercress and radish slivers on a serving platter and top with the fish. Finish off by drizzling over the dressing.

Tray-Baked Chicken

GF DF PP

with Tomato and Fennel

I love a tray bake: you just chuck everything in and leave, and before you know it you will be tucking into this lovely comforting dish. Chicken is high in protein, which makes this a great meal if you do a lot of exercise because it helps with muscle recovery. This goes really well with rice, fresh steamed greens and roasted veggies.

Serves 4

2 large fennel bulbs, cut into ½cm slices

1 red onion, cut into ½cm slices

4 garlic cloves, sliced

2 tbsp avocado oil or melted butter

4 tbsp tomato purée

3 tsp ground cumin

2 tsp fennel seeds

8 sprigs of fresh thyme, leaves picked and finely chopped

1 mild red chilli, finely chopped

2 bay leaves

1 tsp salt

½ tsp freshly ground black pepper

grated zest and juice of 1 lemon

400g can chopped tomatoes

400ml chicken stock

8 chicken thighs with skin on and bone in

For the toppings

2 tbsp chopped fresh parsley

2 tbsp chopped capers

Place all the ingredients apart from the chicken and the toppings in a large bowl and stir well. Add the chicken and stir again. If you have time, leave to marinate overnight in the fridge.

Preheat the oven to 180°C/350°F/gas mark 4. Spread out the chicken thighs and marinade mixture in a large baking tray and put in the oven. Roast for 50 minutes, taking out halfway through to baste the chicken. Remove from the oven and sprinkle over the parsley and capers. Serve hot.

The chicken can be kept in the fridge for 3 days, or frozen to eat at a later date.

Spanish Chickpea Stew
with Chorizo and Spinach

DF S PP 30

This is a recreation of a dish I fell in love with at a tapas restaurant in Tooting. I remember arriving and thinking that it smelt so good. I mean you can't go wrong with anything that's got chorizo in it! I tasted one mouthful and went to heaven. When I got back home, I immediately tried to recreate it. Here's my version – I hope it does the original justice!

Serves 2

1 tbsp olive oil

100g chorizo,
    roughly chopped

1 red onion, finely
    chopped

2 garlic cloves, crushed

1 tsp cumin seeds

1 tsp smoked paprika

salt and freshly ground
    black pepper, to taste

400g can chickpeas,
    drained

2 beef tomatoes,
    roughly chopped

500ml chicken stock

juice of 1 lemon

100g spinach

3 tbsp finely chopped
    fresh flat-leaf parsley

Heat the oil in a large pan and add the chorizo and onion. Cook for 7 minutes until the onion turns golden. Add the garlic, cumin seeds, smoked paprika and a pinch of salt and pepper, and cook for another minute. Tip in the chickpeas and tomatoes and stir well, coating with the spices. Cook for 5 minutes, then pour in the stock and lemon juice and cook for 15 minutes more. When everything is ready, stir through the spinach until it wilts, and sprinkle on the parsley.

Fish Skewers
with Parsnip Chips

GF DF S PP

I love seafood, especially rubbed in my favourite spice, smoked paprika. Teamed with these crunchy, coconut-baked parsnip chips, it brings the taste of holidays to your kitchen. Turn up the tunes and get cooking!

Serves 2–3

200g salmon

200g cod

200g raw prawns

2 tbsp melted coconut oil or avocado oil

2 tsp smoked sweet paprika

1 garlic clove, crushed

1 tbsp tamari

For the parsnip chips

500g parsnips, peeled

2 tbsp coconut oil, avocado oil or butter, melted

3 sprigs of fresh oregano, leaves picked and finely chopped

salt, to taste

Preheat the oven to 180°C/350°F/gas mark 4. Cut the fish into bite-sized chunks and peel the prawns if necessary. Mix together the oil, smoked paprika, garlic and tamari, then add the fish and prawns and stir well. Pop this in the fridge to marinate overnight if you have time.

To make the chips, cut the parsnips into 1cm-thick batons. Mix with the oil, oregano and a good sprinkle of salt then spread out on a large baking tray. Roast in the oven for 45 minutes.

Thread the marinated prawns and fish onto skewers. About 12 minutes before the parsnip chips are done, spread out the skewers on another roasting tray and put in the oven. Bake for 12 minutes until everything is cooked through.

The fish is best eaten on the day, but leftover parsnip chips can be kept for a few days in the fridge.

Maple and Miso Red Rice Salad

(V) GF DF (S) PP

I love red rice – it's nutty, crunchy and holds the flavours of this dish together. Folded into crisp, roasted radishes and broccoli, and mixed with peppery watercress and pecans, red rice is just fantastic. This dish is something I always have in my fridge for a quick, delicious hit.

Serves 4

100g pecans

200g red rice

1 tbsp avocado oil,
    coconut oil or
    melted butter

pinch of salt

100g watercress

**For the roasted radishes
and broccoli**

300g radishes

200g purple sprouting
    tenderstem broccoli

2 tbsp maple syrup

2 tbsp avocado oil,
    coconut oil or
    melted butter

1 tbsp lemon juice

For the miso dressing

2 tbsp miso paste

2 tbsp maple syrup

1 tbsp sesame oil

2 tbsp rice wine vinegar

1 tbsp freshly squeezed
    lemon juice

2 tbsp olive oil

salt and freshly ground
    black pepper, to taste

Preheat the oven to 200°C/400°F/gas mark 6. Heat a small frying pan to a medium–high heat and toast the pecans for 3 minutes, shaking the pan to prevent them burning. Leave to cool on a plate.

Rinse the rice in a sieve under the tap until the water runs clear. Put the oil for the rice into a large pot. Add the rice and stir into the oil with the salt, then pour over 500ml of water and bring to the boil with the lid on. Once the water is boiling, reduce the heat and leave to simmer for 35 minutes (or as per the packet instructions). Fluff up the cooked rice with a fork and leave to sit for 5 minutes with the lid on.

While the rice is cooking, cut the radishes into quarters and slice the purple sprouting broccoli in half lengthways. Place on a roasting tray and drizzle over the maple syrup, oil and lemon juice. Roast in the oven for 25 minutes until golden and cooked through.

Blend or whisk the miso dressing ingredients together. Mix the cooked red rice with the roasted veggies, watercress, miso dressing and toasted pecans. Serve warm.

This salad will last for 2 days in the fridge.

Lamb Chops

with Parsnip Mash and Asparagus

When I think of spring I think of lamb. Rich in vitamin B12 and a high-quality protein, it really is a fantastic meat. Asparagus has a short season but I try and munch on it daily while it's here. These two spring angels go so well with this creamy delicious parsnip mash. Comfort food just got a little bit healthier.

Serves 4

3 tbsp avocado oil or melted butter, plus extra for the griddle pan

grated zest and juice of 1 lemon

2 tbsp capers, finely chopped

2 garlic cloves, crushed

2 sprigs of fresh rosemary, leaves picked and chopped

8 lamb chops

For the parsnip mash

500g parsnips

1 tbsp olive oil

1 tsp mustard

salt and freshly ground black pepper, to taste

For the asparagus

large bunch of asparagus, trimmed

juice of ½ lemon

1 tbsp olive oil

salt, to taste

Make the lamb marinade by mixing the oil, lemon zest and juice, capers, garlic and rosemary together. Add the lamb, coat well and leave to marinate in the fridge for 1 hour.

While this is marinating, make the mash. Peel and chop the parsnips into chunks. Steam over a pan of simmering water for 15 minutes, until cooked through. Drain, then blend or mash until smooth with the olive oil, mustard and a big pinch of salt and pepper. Keep warm until serving.

A little before you are ready to serve, heat a griddle pan for a few minutes until piping hot. Brush some oil over the pan and place the chops and asparagus on the hot griddle. Grill for 3 minutes on each side. Plate up the mash, with the lamb chops on top and asparagus on the side. Pour the lemon juice and olive oil over the asparagus with a sprinkle of salt and serve hot.

Rhubarb and Coconut Rice Pudding

(V) (DF)

I first tried rice pudding on a yoga retreat. It's the most comforting dish; I love it made with Indian spices like cardamom and cinnamon. Rice pudding goes perfectly with stewed rhubarb – and any leftover rhubarb compote is great on top of porridge or on toast at a later date. Pudding rice can be hard to find (trust me, it took some time!) but no worries if you can't find it. Just use short-grain or basmati rice, although check the cooking time for basmati as it cooks a little quicker.

Serves 2

500ml rice milk or
   other milk
200g coconut cream
1 vanilla pod
1 cinnamon stick
1 cardamom pod
1 tbsp maple syrup
120g pudding rice or
   short-grain rice
2 tbsp flaked almonds,
   to serve
extra maple syrup,
   to serve (optional)

For the rhubarb compote

2 rhubarb stalks
2 tbsp maple syrup
grated zest and juice
   of 1 orange

First make the rhubarb compote. Finely chop the rhubarb into 1cm pieces. Place in a saucepan with the maple syrup and orange zest and juice. Bring to the boil, then lower the heat and allow to simmer for 15–20 minutes until cooked through. Keep warm to serve with the rice pudding.

Meanwhile, put the milk, coconut cream, vanilla pod, cinnamon stick, cardamom pod and maple syrup in another pot, over a medium–low heat. Bring to a simmer and cook gently for 10 minutes. Then bring to the boil and add the rice. Cook for 20 minutes, stirring well, until the rice is cooked through. Take out the cinnamon stick, vanilla pod and cardamom pod (if you can find them).

Serve the rice pudding with a dollop of the rhubarb compote and sprinkled with flaked almonds on top, plus a drizzle of maple syrup if needed.

Raw Coconut and Chocolate Bars

V GF DF PP

I've always loved coconuts, and would gorge on shop-bought bars when at school. These, however, are refined sugar free and so easy to make. They last a few weeks in the fridge but if you're like me, they'll all be gone in under 24 hours!

Makes 10 bars

170g desiccated coconut
60g coconut oil, melted
4 tbsp raw honey
pinch of salt
1 tsp vanilla extract

For the almond chocolate coating

90g coconut oil
1¼ tbsp almond butter
40g raw cacao powder
5 tbsp maple syrup
pinch of salt

Mix the desiccated coconut into the melted coconut oil in a bowl, and add the honey, salt and vanilla. Stir well, then tip out on to a baking paper-lined tray and flatten the mixture so it is 1cm high. Freeze for 1 hour.

To make the almond chocolate coating, melt the coconut oil in a small pan over a low heat, then add the almond butter, cacao powder, maple syrup and salt. Give it a good stir together until everything is combined.

Bring the frozen coconut filling out of the freezer and cut into 10 bars. Dip the bars in the melted chocolate coating one at a time and place them on a fresh baking paper-lined tray. Pop back into the freezer for 30 minutes to set, then keep in the fridge until you want to dig in.

Choc Chip and Raisin Blondie Brownies   (V) GF DF PP 30

I love recipes with minimal steps and I know you will love this one. There are no difficult baking techniques, no whisking, no sifting – you just chuck the ingredients together and bake.

Makes 16 bars

2 eggs
1 tsp vanilla extract
1 tsp ground cinnamon
175g cashew nut butter
  or almond butter
120g coconut sugar
1 tsp gluten-free
  bicarbonate of soda
pinch of salt
50g good-quality
  dark chocolate
30g raisins

Preheat the oven to 170°C/325°F/gas mark 3.

Mix together the eggs, vanilla, cinnamon, nut butter, coconut sugar, bicarb and salt in a large bowl until smooth. Break the chocolate into small pieces. Add these chocolate chips and the raisins to the mixture and stir so they're distributed throughout.

Line a 20cm square baking tin with baking paper and pour the mixture into the tin. Bake in the oven for 25 minutes, then leave to cool on a wire rack. Using the paper, remove the brownie slab from the tin. Cut into 16 pieces and enjoy.

The brownies will keep for 3 days in an airtight container (but they will probably last one minute!).

Coffee Pecan Muffins

(V) DF PP 30

These energy boosting muffins work double time. When your mood starts to slump these tasty muffins will pick you up and make the rest of the afternoon plain sailing. Soft in the middle and crunchy on top, they are a pretty irresistible snack!

Makes 6 large muffins

100g pecans, chopped

40g rolled oats

60g spelt or buckwheat flour

1 tsp baking powder

½ tsp bicarbonate of soda

1 tsp ground cinnamon

pinch of salt

50g coconut yogurt or natural yogurt

50g coconut oil or butter, melted and cooled, tplus extra for greasing

1 egg, beaten

1 banana, mashed

4 tbsp date syrup or maple syrup, plus extra to serve

shot of espresso, cooled

Preheat the oven to 200°C/400°F/gas mark 6. Grease a six-hole muffin tray.

Place 50g of pecans in a food processor and grind up. Put the rolled oats, flour, baking powder, bicarb, cinnamon and salt in a mixing bowl and stir in the ground pecans. In a separate bowl, mix the yogurt, oil, egg, banana, syrup and espresso together. Then add the wet mixture to the dry ingredients and mix well together. Pour the batter into the greased muffin tray and top with the rest of the pecans.

Put the muffins in the oven and bake for 18 minutes until risen and cooked through. Leave to cool on a wire rack, then serve with a drizzle of maple syrup.

Keep in an airtight container for 3–4 days.

Summer

Breakfast

Sweetcorn Fritters with Tomato Salsa and Avocado

Four Overnight Oats: Raspberry and Chia, Grilled Peach, Cherry and Chocolate, Berry Nice Zoats

Vegan Banana and Peanut Butter Loaf

Green Shakshuka

Strawberry Basil Smoothie

Sunrise Smoothie

Chilli Scrambled Eggs with Mushrooms on Toast

Soups, Salads and Snacks

Papaya and Peanut Salad

Four Summer Side Salads: Zesty Roasted Radishes, Runner Bean and Toasted Sunflower Seeds, Grated Carrot and Raisin Slaw, Tomatoes with Lemon Zest and Balsamic

Middle Eastern Mezze Bowl

Asian Spiced Mixed Grain Bowl

Avocado Mayo Slaw

Summer Lovin' Bowl

One-Tray Roasted Veg

Two Summer Lunch Boxes: Asparagus, Boiled Egg, Olive and Green Bean Bowl, Potato, Pea, Radish, Brown Rice and Rocket Salad

Two Summer Take-To-Work Snacks: Cannellini Dip with Crudités, Tamari-Roasted Pumpkin Seeds

Mains

Steak Fajitas with Roasted Peppers and Corn

Charred Corn and Tomato Pesto Pasta

Thai Green Chicken Curry

Roasted Cod with Charred Courgettes and Peppers

Whole Spiced Chicken with Baby Cos and Carrots

Pistachio-Crusted Sea Bass with Shaved Fennel and Courgetti

Roasted Aubergine with Tomato Sauce, Quinoa and Toasted Nuts

Dessert

Madeleines

Almond and Blueberry Tart

Three-Ingredient Peaches and Cream Popsicles

Raw Chocolate Peanut Butter Brownie Bites

Sweetcorn Fritters

V DF D PP 15

with Tomato Salsa and Avocado

One of my favourite summer recipes is sweetcorn fritters, which go amazingly with mashed avocado and tomato salsa. Tomatoes really are the superfood of the summer. They're bursting with lycopene, which gives them their beautiful red colour, and has got wonderful benefits for our skin, helping to protect against sunburn, as it has the ability to block UV light. Carry on munching those tomatoes throughout the summer season!

Makes 6 fritters, serves 2

250g uncooked corn kernels

2 eggs

1 garlic clove, crushed

big pinch of salt

½ tsp ground coriander

½ tsp ground cumin

½ tsp smoked paprika

½ tsp baking powder

2 spring onions, chopped

3 tbsp chopped fresh coriander

3 tbsp porridge oats

1 tbsp coconut oil

1 avocado, pitted, peeled and sliced

1 lime, cut into wedges

For the tomato salsa

½ red chilli, deseeded and finely chopped

1 beef tomato, diced

1 tbsp chopped fresh basil

¼ red onion, finely chopped

1 tbsp olive oil

1 tsp red wine vinegar

pinch of salt

Place three quarters of the corn in a food processor along with the eggs, garlic and salt. Blend until smooth. Add the rest of the corn, the spices, baking powder, spring onions, fresh coriander and oats, and process for 10 seconds. Then pour the fritter mixture into a bowl.

Melt the coconut oil in a small frying pan over a medium heat. Pour 2 tablespoons of mixture into the pan to form a fritter. Fry for 3 minutes on one side, then flip over and cook for another minute until cooked through. Transfer to a plate. Repeat with the rest of the mixture to make 6 fritters.

To make the salsa, mix all the ingredients together in a small bowl.

Serve the fritters with slices of avocado, the salsa and wedges of lime to squeeze over.

Four Overnight Oats

Overnight oats are awesome all year round but best on a warm day. As well as making a really quick and easy breakfast, they contain tocotrienols, which are part of the vitamin E family. You're probably thinking what on earth are tocotrienols?! Well, they are capable of reducing the penetration of UV radiation, which is awesome news in the summer. I love popping oats in Tupperware and making a few batches at a time – here are a few of my favourites!

Raspberry and Chia

Serves 1

V DF I5

75g porridge oats
250ml almond milk or other milk
75g raspberries, plus extra to serve
1 tbsp chia seeds
1 tbsp pumpkin seeds
maple syrup, to serve

Mix the oats, milk, raspberries, chia seeds and pumpkin seeds together in a bowl and leave in the fridge overnight to soak. Eat in the morning with a few more raspberries on top and a drizzle of maple syrup.

Grilled Peach

Serves 1

V DF I5

75g porridge oats
200ml almond or oat milk
1 tsp vanilla extract
3 dried apricots
1 peach
1 tbsp coconut oil
1 tbsp honey

Mix the oats, milk and vanilla together. Leave to soak for 15 minutes if eating immediately. Chop up the apricots into thin slivers and stir in. Remove the stone from the peach and slice thinly. Heat the coconut oil in a griddle pan over a medium heat, and grill the peach slices for a few minutes on each side so they are cooked through. Place the peaches on top of the oat mixture and drizzle over the honey. Leave in the fridge overnight to eat cold the next day, or eat immediately while the peaches are still warm.

Serves 1

75g porridge oats
1 tbsp raw cacao powder
1 tsp raw cacao nibs
220ml rice or almond milk
1 tbsp maple syrup
50g cherries, stoned
   and chopped, plus
   extra to serve
small pinch of salt
1 tsp toasted desiccated
   coconut, plus extra
   to serve

Cherry and Chocolate

V DF 15

Mix everything apart from the desiccated coconut and extra cherries together in a bowl. Sprinkle over the coconut and leave in the fridge overnight. Serve the next morning with a few more cherries on top and another sprinkle of coconut for extra flavour.

Serves 1

50g porridge oats
½ courgette, grated
250ml almond or
   rice milk
½ tsp vanilla extract
1 tsp flaxseeds
50g blueberries
½ tsp ground cinnamon
3 tbsp natural yogurt,
   to serve
1 tbsp maple syrup,
   to serve

Berry Nice Zoats

V 15

Place everything apart from the yogurt and maple syrup in a bowl, stir well and leave overnight to soak up the liquid. Drizzle over the yogurt and maple syrup in the morning.

Vegan Banana and Peanut Butter Loaf

(V) (PP)

We all love banana loaf but I've taken this up a notch by adding peanut butter. Oh yes, bananas are a great source of energy, but did you know they can also help you to sleep? Whenever I want a really good night's sleep I'll munch on this loaf because bananas contain trytophan, an amino acid that helps the body to produce serotonin. It calms and relaxes you, which is essential for glowing skin!

Makes 1 medium loaf

coconut oil, for greasing
  (optional)
80ml maple syrup
3 ripe bananas, mashed
100g coconut oil, melted
1 tsp vanilla extract
80g coconut sugar
200g spelt flour or
  gluten-free flour
1 tbsp chia seeds
1 tsp baking powder
½ tsp bicarbonate of soda
pinch of salt
150g good-quality
  chocolate, chopped into
  small chunks or chips
125g peanut butter or
  almond butter

Preheat the oven to 170°C/325°F/gas mark 3. Grease a loaf tin with coconut oil or line with baking paper.

Put the maple syrup, mashed banana, coconut oil, vanilla and sugar in a large bowl and mix well. In another bowl, stir together the flour, chia seeds, baking powder, bicarb and salt. Tip the flour mixture into the wet mixture in the first bowl and stir together well. Pour a quarter of the batter into the prepared loaf tin, then sprinkle a quarter of the chocolate chips over and dot a quarter of the nut butter on top in teaspoons. Repeat this layering with the rest of the mixture.

Bake in the oven for 50 minutes until just cooked through and golden on top. You want this cake to be moist. Remove from the loaf tin and leave to cool on a wire rack, then slice and enjoy.

Green Shakshuka

V GF D PP 30

You've probably heard of baked eggs. The Middle Eastern version is called shakshuka, and it's full of flavour! This version is green, bursting with herbs that thrive in the summer like parsley and coriander. Fennel is really soothing on the stomach and digestive system so if you're looking for something to beat the bloat in the summer this is your ideal breakfast!

Serves 2

½ tsp cumin seeds

2 tbsp avocado oil

1 large red onion,
   finely diced

2 green peppers, deseeded
   and finely chopped

1 fennel bulb, finely
   chopped

1 bay leaf

2 sprigs of fresh thyme,
   leaves picked and
   chopped

1 tbsp chopped fresh
   flat-leaf parsley

2 tbsp chopped fresh
   coriander

1 small courgette, grated

pinch of cayenne pepper

100ml veggie stock

salt and freshly ground
   black pepper, to taste

4 eggs

100g feta cheese

2 tbsp toasted pine nuts

rye or sourdough bread,
   to serve

olives, to serve

Toast the cumin seeds in a large saucepan over a medium heat for 1 minute until they become fragrant, shaking the pan to prevent them burning. Add the oil and onion, and sauté for 5 minutes until golden. Put the green peppers, fennel, bay leaf, thyme, parsley and half the coriander into the pan, and continue cooking for another 5 minutes. Then add the courgette, cayenne and stock. Turn down the heat to low and simmer for 15 minutes. Taste and add salt and pepper as necessary.

Place two fresh saucepans over a medium heat and divide the veggie mixture between them. Break two eggs into each pan, fitting them into gaps in the mixture. Sprinkle the eggs with a little salt, cover and cook very gently for 6–7 minutes, until the egg whites are cooked through but the yolks are still runny. Crumble over the feta and sprinkle on the remaining chopped coriander, a pinch of salt and the toasted pine nuts. Serve with rye bread and olives.

Strawberry Basil Smoothie

(V) GF DF 15

Serves 1

300ml rice or almond milk

200g strawberries, hulled

1 tsp vanilla extract

3 fresh basil leaves

1 tbsp lemon juice

1 Medjool date or soft date, pitted

2 ice cubes

Basil with strawberry – you're probably thinking I've gone mad but the sweet fresh taste of basil actually goes really well with strawberries. Strawberries are my favourite summer fruit and a serving of these berries has more Vitamin C than an orange! This smoothie reminds me of Wimbledon – think strawberries and cream with a twist.

Place everything in a blender and whizz until smooth.

Sunrise Smoothie

(V) GF DF (S) 15

Serves 1

1 orange

1 banana

½ mango

1 Medjool or soft date, pitted

½ tsp freshly grated ginger

1 tbsp chia seeds

½ tsp vanilla extract

200ml coconut milk

I prefer to eat light in summer, and this refreshing smoothie is just the thing. Packed full of vitamin-rich fruit, it keeps you full throughout the day thanks to the fibre found in the chia seeds. They also add a nice bit of crunch.

Peel and stone the fruit. Place everything in a blender and whizz until smooth.

Chilli Scrambled Eggs

V DF D PP 15

with Mushrooms on Toast

There's no better way to start the day than with eggs. Sometimes I like to mix things up by adding chilli. Chillies are high in beta-carotene, which turns into vitamin A in the body. It really revs up our immune system and helps give you the summer skin you've always dreamed of.

Serves 2

200g mushrooms

2 tbsp avocado oil
 or butter

salt, to taste

sprig of fresh thyme, leaves
 picked and chopped

4 eggs

1 mild red chilli, finely
 chopped

2 slices of rye or
 sourdough bread

Finely slice the mushrooms. Heat 1 tablespoon of the oil in a frying pan and sauté the mushrooms with a pinch of salt and the thyme for 7 minutes until cooked through.

While the mushrooms are cooking, whisk the eggs in a large bowl with a fork. Add a pinch of salt and half of the chopped chilli. Heat the other tablespoon of oil in a second pan and wait for it to get hot. Pour the beaten eggs into the pan and let them sit for 10 seconds, then with a wooden spoon move the outer edges of the egg towards the middle. Repeat around all the edges so the uncooked egg gets pushed into the empty part of the pan, and keep doing this until the egg is 80% cooked.

Toast your chosen bread and spoon over the mushrooms, then put the eggs on top. Serve with an extra sprinkling of chopped chilli if you like a kick.

Papaya and Peanut Salad

(V) (GF) (DF) (PP) I5

Papaya is a gorgeous juicy orange fruit that reminds me of when I went on safari. We watched the sunset by a lake, cooked up a BBQ and had this delicious papaya salad as a side dish. I've recreated this amazing summer salad just for you. Papaya is great for the digestion and has the most heavenly taste.

**Serves 2 as a main
or 4 as a side**

1 small papaya
200g sugar snap peas
2 spring onions, finely
   chopped
2 tbsp finely chopped
   fresh basil
2 little gem lettuces,
   finely chopped
50g toasted peanuts

For the dressing

juice of 1 lime
1 tbsp tamari
1 tbsp freshly grated ginger
1 tbsp tahini
1 tbsp maple syrup

Peel, deseed and cut the papaya into thin slices. Slice the sugar snap peas diagonally into thin strips. Whisk the dressing ingredients together. Mix the papaya, sugar snaps, spring onions, basil and lettuces together with the peanuts. Pour over the dressing and serve.

Four Summer Side Salads

Zesty Roasted Radishes

V GF DF 30

Serves 2

200g radishes
2 tbsp avocado oil or
   melted butter
2 sprigs of fresh thyme
salt and freshly ground
   black pepper, to taste
grated zest and juice
   of ½ lemon

Radishes are one of my favourite vegetables to eat raw. They're so crunchy and refreshing, I can't wait for summer to come around so that I can get my hands on gorgeous fresh ones! Pop them in a salad for a spicy crunch and a burst of antioxidant vitamin C!

Preheat the oven to 200°C/400°F/gas mark 6. Cut the radishes into quarters and place on a roasting tray. Pour over the oil and add the thyme, a big pinch of salt and pepper, the lemon zest and 1 tablespoon of the lemon juice. Roast for 20–25 minutes until cooked through.

Runner Bean and Toasted Sunflower Seeds

V GF DF 15 S

Serves 2

2 tbsp sunflower seeds
400g runner beans or
   French beans, trimmed
½ small shallot,
   finely minced
2 tbsp olive oil
1 tbsp lemon juice
pinch of salt

I'm all about crowding greens into my diet – they fill me up and super-charge my body. Sunflower seeds are magical too. They contain huge amounts of vitamin E, which is incredibly moisturising for the skin, so with the sun coming out and holidays booked make sure you throw these babies over your salads to keep your skin radiant.

Heat a small frying pan to a medium–high heat and toast the sunflower seeds for 1–2 minutes, shaking the pan to prevent them burning. Transfer to a plate and leave on the side to cool.

Steam the beans over a pan of simmering water for 3–4 minutes until just cooked through. Put the shallot, olive oil, lemon juice and salt in a small bowl and whisk together well. Toss the beans in the dressing and top with the toasted sunflower seeds.

1 tbsp rice vinegar

2 tbsp lime juice

1 tbsp maple syrup

salt, to taste

300g carrots, grated

2 spring onions, finely
chopped

2 tbsp finely chopped
fresh coriander

½ jalapeño chilli,
deseeded and chopped
(or to taste)

75g raisins

Grated Carrot and Raisin Slaw   V GF DF 15

Remember the old wives' tale that carrots help you see in the dark? Well, as well as being super satisfying to munch on, they protect us from UVB radiation with carotenoids – antioxidants that reduce the negative effects of UVB. Your salad will brighten your day and get that added sweetness from the bursts of raisins!

Whisk the vinegar, lime juice and maple syrup together with a big pinch of salt. Mix the grated carrots, spring onions, coriander, jalapeño and raisins together in a bowl. Dress the salad, then sprinkle over a little extra salt and serve.

This slaw will keep for 3 days in the fridge.

Serves 2

200g beef tomatoes

grated zest and juice
of ½ lemon

3 tbsp olive oil

1 tbsp balsamic vinegar

salt and freshly ground
black pepper, to taste

Tomatoes with Lemon Zest and Balsamic   V GF DF 15

Tomatoes are great for SPF protection from the lycopene they contain, which gives them their colour. I love tomatoes because you can get them in all different sizes. I often pop small ones in my bag for a snack, but when I'm looking for a showstopping salad, the bigger the better!

Cut the tomatoes into 1cm slices and put on a serving dish. Sprinkle the lemon zest over the tomatoes. Whisk the olive oil, balsamic and 1 tablespoon of the lemon juice together with a big pinch of salt and pepper and pour over the tomatoes.

Middle Eastern Mezze Bowl

 V GF PP 30

I love anything in a bowl. It sounds silly but food just tastes better in one! There are so many flavours going on in this dish, I just can't resist it. Middle Eastern cuisine is rich in vegetables, fruits, grains and fish, and most of the fats consumed are unsaturated, from things like olive oil and nuts. Get gorgeous glowing skin from this tasty dish and transport yourself to the Middle East with every bite.

Serves 2

1 aubergine
3 tbsp avocado oil or
   melted butter
salt and freshly ground
   black pepper, to taste
100g quinoa
1 avocado
juice of ½ a lemon,
   for the avocado
1 small cucumber
100g Kalamata olives
2 tbsp chopped
   fresh parsley

For the dressing

3 tbsp natural yogurt
1 tbsp tahini
1½ tbsp lemon juice
¼ tsp ground cumin
pinch of salt

Slice the aubergine into thin strips, place in a bowl and pour over the oil, then sprinkle with plenty of salt and pepper. Heat a griddle pan to a medium heat. Once the pan is hot, griddle the aubergine slices in batches, for 4 minutes each side, until cooked through. Put to one side to cool.

Rinse the quinoa in a sieve, then place in a pot with 250ml of water and a pinch of salt. Bring to the boil, then let it simmer for 12 minutes until all the water has been soaked up and the quinoa is cooked through.

Peel, stone and thinly slice the avocado. Cover the slices in the lemon juice so as not to brown. Slice the cucumber into 1cm chunks. Divide the prepped mezze items and the olives between your two bowls, but keep everything separate. Whisk the dressing ingredients together and drizzle on top, then sprikle with the chopped parsley.

Asian Spiced Mixed Grain Bowl

(V) GF DF (S) (PP) (15)

The tahini dressing in this dish really goes well with all of the Asian flavours that are added to the grains. Tahini is amazing for vegetarian and plant-based diets because it's got an extremely high calcium content. Mixed with tamari, it makes the best summer salad dressing!

Serves 4

100g red rice
100g white quinoa
1 tbsp coconut oil
1 red onion, finely
    chopped
2 garlic cloves, crushed
1 tbsp freshly grated ginger
1 red chilli, deseeded and
    finely chopped
1 tbsp tamari
2 pak choi, finely chopped

For the dressing

2 tbsp tahini
2 tbsp olive oil
1 tbsp tamari
juice of 1 lemon
1 garlic clove, crushed
2 tsp freshly grated ginger

Rinse then cook the rice and quinoa separately as per the packet instructions.

Heat the coconut oil in a frying pan and sauté the onion for 7 minutes. Add the garlic, ginger, chilli and tamari and cook for another 2 minutes. Throw in the pak choi and cooked grains, stir, and cook for a further 2 minutes, warming everything through.

Whisk the dressing ingredients together. Plate up the grain salad, pour over the dressing and dig in.

Avocado 'Mayo' Slaw

(V) GF DF (S) PP 15

Mayo can be pretty stodgy but this avocado mayo is light, refreshing and bursting with green goodness – without losing that lovely creaminess. Teamed with the crunchy vegetables, this slaw is made for a summer's day.

Serves 4 as a side

2 carrots, julienned

2 fennel bulbs, julienned

2 red peppers, deseeded and julienned

200g radishes, julienned

1 mild red chilli, deseeded and finely chopped

50g toasted cashews, chopped

For the avo mayo

2 avocados, peeled and stoned

4 tbsp olive oil

1 tbsp lemon juice

½ tsp garlic powder

2 tsp Dijon mustard

1 tsp salt

First make the avocado mayo. Put the avocados, olive oil, lemon juice, garlic powder, mustard and salt in a blender or food processor and blend together until smooth. Then mix together the prepped veggies and chilli in a bowl and stir through the avocado cream. Top with the toasted nuts to serve.

Summer Lovin' Bowl

(V) GF DF PP

My favourite film of all time is *Grease* . . . so you can see where the name comes from. This is basically a combination of all the things I love about summer. It's a real mixture of things, but it really packs a punch. Say hello to flavour and goodbye to soggy lettuce in Tupperware, and take this to work instead!

Serves 2

2 large beetroots

1 tbsp avocado oil or melted coconut oil

salt and freshly ground black pepper, to taste

100g buckwheat

1 cucumber, chopped into 1cm chunks

1 mango, peeled, stoned and chopped into 1cm chunks

juice of 1 lime

2 tbsp chopped fresh coriander

1 jalapeño chilli, deseeded

4 tbsp hummus

1 tbsp chopped walnuts

For the dressing

2 tbsp almond butter

1 tbsp olive oil

1 tbsp lemon juice

1 tsp nutritional yeast (if you can find it)

1 tsp tamari

pinch of chilli powder

pinch of smoked paprika

1 tbsp cold water

Preheat the oven to 200°C/400°F/gas mark 6.

Peel and cut the beetroots into 2½cm chunks. Put in a roasting tray and mix with the oil and a big pinch of salt and pepper. Roast for 30–40 minutes until cooked through.

While the beetroots are cooking, cook the buckwheat and make the dressing. First rinse the buckwheat in warm water, then place in a pot with 250ml of cold water and a pinch of salt. Bring to the boil and simmer for 12 minutes until cooked through and all the water has been absorbed. Whisk the dressing ingredients together.

Mix the cucumber, mango and lime juice together with the coriander and jalapeño. Plate up the roasted beets with the cooked buckwheat, hummus and walnuts, plus the cucumber and mango salad. Drizzle over the dressing.

One-Tray Roasted Veg

V GF DF

This is the perfect way to use up leftover veg. It's a brilliant mix of yummy summer veggies that will deliver lots of vitamins and minerals straight to your beautiful body. It's so quick and easy to chuck on to a roasting tray, why not whip this up for a fuss-free summer side dish or at the beginning of the week to keep in the fridge for when you're low on time.

Serves 4 as a side

2 red onions

2 courgettes

1 cauliflower, leaves removed

grated zest of ½ orange

grated zest of ½ lemon

juice of 1 lemon

1 tbsp maple syrup

½ red chilli, deseeded and chopped

4 sprigs of fresh thyme, leaves picked and chopped

2 tbsp avocado oil or melted coconut oil

salt, to taste

1 orange, peeled and cut into segments

1 tbsp olive oil

For the tahini dressing

3 tbsp tahini

1½ tsp maple syrup

2 tsp lemon juice

3 tbsp water

½ tsp salt

Preheat the oven to 200°C/400°F/gas mark 6.

Thinly slice the red onions, cut the courgettes into 2½cm chunks and chop the cauliflower into small florets. Mix the veggies together in a bowl with the orange and lemon zests, lemon juice, maple syrup, chilli, thyme and avocado or coconut oil. Sprinkle on plenty of salt and pepper, then spread out on a roasting tray. Roast in the oven for 40 minutes until cooked through.

Whisk the tahini dressing together. Mix the orange segments in with the roasted veggies, drizzle with the olive oil and serve with the tahini dressing.

Two Summer Lunch Boxes

Lunch box dishes are the most requested recipes on my blog. There is nothing better than having a delicious home-made lunch to tuck into at work rather than heading to the supermarket to pick out that same old sandwich. These lunch box recipes are light, tasty and keep well in your Tupperware.

Asparagus, Boiled Egg, Olive and Green Bean Bowl

V · GF · DF · D · PP · 15

Serves 1

100g asparagus, trimmed
100g green beans
2 eggs
100g olives, pitted and chopped
1 tsp sesame seeds

For the dressing

1 tbsp olive oil
1 tsp apple cider vinegar
1 tsp mustard
pinch of salt

Steam the asparagus and green beans over a pan of simmering water for 4 minutes, then drain. Meanwhile, in another pot, boil the eggs in plenty of water for 5–6 minutes, until just cooked through. Once cool enough to handle, peel the eggs and halve. Whisk the dressing ingredients together in a small container. Roughly chop the olives and add to a lunch box together with the asparagus, green beans and sesame seeds. Pour over the dressing when ready to eat.

Potato, Pea, Radish, Brown Rice and Rocket Salad

V · GF · DF · 15

Serves 1

1 tbsp tahini
1 tsp tamari
juice of ½ lime
½ tsp chilli flakes
50g baby new potatoes, boiled
4 radishes, sliced
70g cooked brown rice
25g rocket
50g frozen peas, defrosted

Whisk the tahini, tamari, lime juice, chilli flakes and 1 tablespoon of water together. Tip this dressing into a small container to keep separate from the salad.

Cut the potatoes in half, put in a bowl and add the radishes, brown rice, rocket and peas. Mix together and put in your lunch box. Keep everything in the fridge, then at lunchtime, pour the dressing over your salad and enjoy.

Two Summer Take-to-Work Snacks

A handful of these deliciously crunchy roasted pumpkin seeds will stop the munchies in no time. Packed full of spot-zapping zinc, pumpkin seeds are the key to clear, glowing skin. Another one of my favourite summer snacks is this super simple and deliciously creamy cannellini dip. Watch out – it's the next hummus!

Cannellini Dip with Crudités

V **GF** **DF** **15**

Serves 8

400g can cannellini beans, rinsed and drained
1 garlic clove
10g fresh basil
1 tsp tamari
1 tbsp freshly grated ginger
1 tsp salt
juice of 1 lime
5 tbsp olive oil

For the crudités

1 cucumber, cut into batons
2 carrots, cut into batons
1 fennel bulb, sliced
100g cherry tomatoes, halved
100g radishes, halved

Put the cannellini beans in a food processor with the garlic, basil, tamari, ginger, salt and lime juice. Process until smooth, while slowly pouring in the olive oil a little at a time. Serve with the chopped crudités.

The bean dip will last for up to a week in the fridge.

Tamari-Roasted Pumpkin Seeds

V **GF** **DF** **S** **15**

Serves 3

1 tsp coconut oil
50g pumpkin seeds
1 tsp tamari
½ tsp chilli flakes

Heat the oil in a pan over a medium–high heat and add the pumpkin seeds, tamari and chilli flakes. Stir well so the seeds are evenly covered and cook for 3 minutes until they turn golden, stirring regularly. Take off the heat and transfer to a plate to cool. Once cool and crunchy, place in an airtight container until snack time.

Steak Fajitas

DF D PP

with Roasted Peppers and Corn

If you've got my book *Ready Steady Glow*, you might have tried my chicken fajitas. I love mixing it up with beef because grass-fed beef is a brilliant source of omega 3 fatty acids. Grab your favourite wraps, invite your friends over and have a fajita night!

Serves 4

4 x 150g ribeye steaks
4 corn on the cob ears
2 yellow peppers
1 tbsp avocado oil
    or butter
8 tortilla wraps
1 little gem lettuce
1 lime, cut into wedges
1 tbsp chopped fresh
    coriander

For the marinade

4 tbsp avocado oil
    or olive oil
1 tsp dried chilli powder
1 tsp smoked paprika
2 tsp ground cumin
grated zest and juice
    of 1 lime
big pinch of salt

Make the marinade by mixing together the oil, spices, lime zest and juice and salt. Add the steaks and corn on the cob, coat in the mixture and leave to marinate in the fridge for at least 2 hours, overnight if possible.

Separate out the steaks and roll each ear of corn in foil. Deseed and slice the peppers into thin strips. Heat the oil in a large griddle pan over a medium–high heat, or brush the BBQ with oil. Griddle the pepper strips for 10 minutes until cooked through. Then pop in the corn on the cob and cook in their foil for 10 minutes, turning every minute. Remove the foil and cook for another few minutes until they start to char.

Move the peppers and corn to a plate, then griddle the steaks for 2 minutes each side so they're still rare in the middle. Leave to rest for a few minutes, then cut into thin slices. Shave the corn kernels from the cob and shred the lettuce.

To enjoy, grab a tortilla and chuck in some corn, lettuce, peppers and steak. Squeeze on some lime juice and sprinkle over some coriander.

Charred Corn and Tomato Pesto Pasta   Ⓥ GF DF Ⓢ 30

Brown rice pasta is a brilliant, more natural version of gluten-free pasta. I love it because it is the closest thing to the real deal. It's also great at soaking up the gorgeous flavours of any sauce. Packed with body-loving veggies, this dish will get your skin radiant in no time.

Serves 2

150g brown rice pasta
2 corn on the cob ears
1 tbsp coconut oil or melted butter
1 tsp smoked paprika
2 garlic cloves, crushed
50g sun-dried tomatoes, chopped
50g spinach

For the pesto

25g fresh basil leaves
100g toasted pine nuts
big pinch of salt
½ tsp garlic powder
1 tsp dried chilli flakes
juice of 1 lemon
50ml olive oil

Cook the pasta as per the packet instructions, drain and leave to the side. Next make the pesto. In a blender or food processor, whizz together the basil, pine nuts, salt, garlic powder, chilli flakes and lemon juice. Slowly add the olive oil as you blend, until smooth.

Rub the corn in the oil, then in the smoked paprika and garlic. Heat a griddle pan to a high heat and put in the corn. Griddle for 15 minutes, turning every few minutes, until the corn is cooked through.

Allow the corn to cool slightly, then, using a sharp knife, cut off the kernels. Place in a large pan with the pasta, 4 tablespoons of the pesto, the sun-dried tomatoes and spinach. Put over a low heat and cook until the spinach wilts and the pesto is warmed through. Serve hot.

Keep the rest of the pesto for up to 5 days in the fridge for dips and for adding to other dishes such as the Roasted Cod with Charred Courgettes and Peppers (see page 120) or Whole Spiced Chicken with Baby Cos and Carrots (see page 123).

Thai Green Chicken Curry

GF DF PP 30

There are so many colourful vegetables available in the summer and we've got to make the most of them while they're around! In this recipe I'm using a delicious mix of veg like sweetcorn, mangetout, cherry tomatoes, courgette and basil, packed with our free-radical-fighting and skin-protecting antioxidant friends.

Serves 4

2 tbsp coconut oil
    or butter

500g chicken breasts or
    thighs, chopped into
    2½cm strips

pinch of salt

2 corn on the cob ears

2 garlic cloves, crushed

1 tbsp freshly grated ginger

3 tbsp green Thai curry
    paste

100g cherry tomatoes,
    halved

400ml can coconut milk

1 tbsp tamari

200g mangetout

4 courgettes, spiralised

1 red chilli, deseeded
    and finely chopped

2 tbsp chopped fresh basil

juice of 1 lime

Heat I tablespoon of the oil in a large pot over a medium–high heat, add the chicken and a pinch of salt and cook for 5 minutes. Once the chicken has browned, remove from the pot and leave to one side.

Remove the kernels from the corn ears. Put the remaining oil in the pot, turn down the heat to medium and add the corn kernels. Sauté for 2 minutes, then add the garlic, ginger, curry paste and tomatoes. Stir for a minute until fragrant, then add the coconut milk, tamari and mangetout. Cook for 5 minutes, then put the chicken back in and add the spiralised courgette and cook for a further 5 minutes.

Sprinkle on the chopped chilli and basil and squeeze over some fresh lime juice before serving. This goes really well with a side of brown rice.

Roasted Cod
with Charred Courgettes and Peppers

GF DF PP

It wouldn't be summer without a BBQ! I love trying new flavours on the BBQ – trust me, ditch the shop-bought sausages and burgers and cook up this flavour-rich cod that will make your skin glow, fill you up and keep you satisfied. Enjoy with an evening of sun, and good friends by your side!

Serves 2

2 x 150g cod fillets
salt, to taste
2 courgettes
2 red peppers
2 tbsp avocado oil
  or olive oil
grated zest and juice
  of 1 lemon

For the marinade

2 tbsp chopped fresh
  coriander
1 garlic clove, crushed
1 tsp tomato concentrate
1 tsp apple cider vinegar
1 tsp freshly grated ginger
1 tbsp tamari
pinch of allspice

First make the marinade by combining all the ingredients. Next take the cod fillets and sprinkle on a little salt, then rub three quarters of the marinade into them. Leave to marinate overnight if possible.

Heat the BBQ or a griddle pan to a medium–high heat. Slice the courgettes lengthways into 1½cm-thick strips. Deseed and slice the peppers. Brush the courgette and pepper strips in 1 tablespoon of the oil and sprinkle on a pinch of salt. Grill for a few minutes on each side until cooked through and golden. Leave them to one side.

Heat a frying pan to a high heat with the remaining tablespoon of oil. Place the cod in the pan, skin side down, and cook for 5 minutes, then flip it over for another 3–4 minutes until cooked through.

Add 1 teaspoon of the lemon zest, half the lemon juice, a pinch of salt and the rest of the marinade to the grilled veggies and mix well. Plate up the dressed veggies with the cod on top and serve with the rest of the fresh lemon juice squeezed over.

Whole Spiced Chicken
with Baby Cos and Carrots

GF DF PP

What is a week without a Sunday roast? I know I love enjoying a roast all year round, so here's my summer version that is light on the tummy and packed with gorgeous veggies like little gem lettuce, fennel and carrots!

Serves 4–6

1 x 1.8kg organic whole
    chicken
500g carrots
2 fennel bulbs
1 tbsp avocado oil
salt and freshly ground
    black pepper, to taste
1 little gem lettuce

For the marinade

1 tbsp smoked paprika
½ tsp cayenne pepper
½ tsp garlic powder
grated zest and juice
    of 1 lemon
1 tsp salt
2 tbsp avocado oil
    or melted butter

Mix the marinade ingredients together and rub into the chicken. If you can, leave the chicken overnight in the fridge to marinate.

Preheat the oven to 220°C/425°F/gas mark 7, or as high as it goes.

Place the marinated chicken in a large roasting tray. Cut the carrots into sixths lengthwise and position around the chicken. Cut the fennel into sixths and place around the carrots. Drizzle the oil over the veggies and sprinkle on plenty of salt and pepper. Put the tray in the oven and immediately reduce the temperature to 180°C/350°F/gas mark 4. Cook for 1 hour and 20 minutes, until the chicken's juices run clear.

Just before the chicken is done, slice the gem lettuce into quarters. Take the chicken out and let it rest for 5 minutes. Place the little gem in amongst the veggies and pop back in the oven for another 5 minutes to crisp up. Serve all together warm.

Pistachio-Crusted Sea Bass

GF DF PP 15

with Shaved Fennel and Courgetti

Sea bass is one of my favourite types of fish. Fish doesn't have to be cooked on its own –
I love adding as much flavour as possible. A pistachio crust is the perfect addition and, amongst
other things, pistachios aid digestion. Mixed with super-tummy-soothing fennel, you've got a
winning dish if you need something light.

Serves 2

25g chopped pistachios
25g fresh basil
1 tbsp lemon juice
1 tsp lemon zest
salt, to taste
3 tbsp olive oil
2 x 150g sea bass fillets
1 fennel bulb
2 courgettes
lemon wedges, to serve

Preheat the oven to 180°C/350°F/gas mark 4.

In a blender or food processor, blend the pistachios, basil, lemon juice, zest,
a big pinch of salt and the olive oil until fully combined. Place the sea bass
on a roasting tray and slash the surface before rubbing a little salt and three
quarters of the pistachio mixture into the fish.

Put the sea bass in the oven and roast for 7–8 minutes (depending on
size) until it is cooked through and the flesh is opaque when pierced with
a knife. While the fish is cooking, use a mandolin or sharp knife to slice the
fennel into thin layers, and spiralise the courgettes into noodles. Mix with
the rest of the pistachio mixture and plate up the veg.

Once the fish is ready, place the fish on top of the fennel and courgetti.
Serve with some fresh lemon juice squeezed over.

Roasted Aubergine

(V) GF DF S PP

with Tomato Sauce, Quinoa and Toasted Nuts

The mighty aubergine is a sponge, as it soaks in all the flavours you team it with. In Mediterranean countries you often see aubergine plants growing by the side of the road, so fresh it makes you want to have a vegetable patch. Through the summer months it's got this awesome deep flavour, and it's a very cooling food as it has the ability to clear heat and toxins from the body.

Serves 4

2 large aubergines
salt, to taste
5 tbsp olive oil
50g pistachios
50g flaked almonds
150g quinoa
grated zest and juice
    of 1 lemon
½ tsp dried chilli flakes
2 tbsp chopped fresh
    parsley
2 tbsp chopped fresh
    coriander

For the tomato sauce

2 tbsp olive oil
1 white onion, chopped
1 tsp salt
4 garlic cloves, crushed
1 tsp dried oregano
⅓ tsp dried thyme
1 tsp dried chilli flakes
2 x 400g cans tomatoes
4 sun-dried tomatoes,
    chopped

Make the tomato sauce first. Heat the oil in a large frying pan and sauté the onion with the salt for 7 minutes until golden. Add the garlic, oregano, thyme and chilli flakes and stir for a minute. Then add both types of tomatoes, turn down the heat and simmer for 30 minutes.

While the sauce is cooking, preheat the oven to 200°C/400°F/gas mark 6.

Cut the aubergines in half lengthways, score them on the inside and place them in a roasting tray. Cover in a sprinkling of salt and 4 tablespoons of the oil, and pour over the tomato sauce. Rub the sauce into the aubergine flesh. Roast in the oven for 45–50 minutes until cooked through.

While the aubergines are cooking, toast the nuts. Heat a small frying pan to a medium–high heat and add the pistachios and almonds. Toast for a few minutes until golden, shaking the pan to prevent them burning, then leave on a plate to the side to cool.

Rinse the quinoa in a sieve, then put in a large pot and cover with 380ml of water. Add a pinch of salt and bring to the boil, then simmer for 12 minutes until all the liquid is absorbed. Mix the cooked quinoa with the lemon zest and juice, chilli flakes, chopped herbs and the remaining tablespoon of oil.

Once the aubergine halves are roasted, plate up, topped with the quinoa mixture and the toasted nuts.

Madeleines

V GF DF 30

It's not a coincidence that I love madeleines. My love for these soft shell-shaped sponges blossomed at a young age, but I also lived in France for a brief time when I returned from Australia. I'd just set up my blog, and was experimenting with how to make some of my favourite treats gluten, dairy and refined sugar free. Well, I finally did it with the madeleines, but I have to say I'm yet to crack the croissant!

Makes 16, serves 6–8

50g coconut oil, melted, plus extra for greasing
60ml almond milk
85g maple syrup or honey
grated zest of 1 lemon
1 egg, beaten
1 tsp vanilla extract
120g buckwheat or white spelt flour
1 tsp baking powder
¼ tsp bicarbonate of soda

For the strawberry chia jam

400g strawberries
4 tsp chia seeds
3 tbsp maple syrup

Preheat the oven to 190°C/375°F/gas mark 5 and brush a madeleine tray with melted coconut oil.

Make the jam by blending the strawberries, chia seeds and maple syrup until smooth. Leave on the side – the chia seeds will soak up the liquid and the mixture will become gelatinous after 10 minutes.

To make the madeleines, whisk the coconut oil, almond milk, maple syrup, lemon zest, egg and vanilla together in a large bowl. Sift in the flour, baking powder and bicarb and stir to mix. Pour the batter into the madeleine moulds and bake in the oven for 10 minutes.

Serve the madeleines with a dollop of jam. They are also great dipped in chocolate.

Almond and Blueberry Tart

V GF DF

I adore blueberries. They taste awesome in breakfast dishes but they also make a particularly great tart. Try this one out in the summer months: berries are alkaline and cooling, so it's perfect on a summer day. It will also give your skin a boost with the vitamin E from the almonds and omega 3 from the chia seeds, making this tart not only indulgent but nourishing.

Serves 8

50g coconut oil or butter,
    plus extra for greasing
2 tbsp maple syrup
1 tsp vanilla extract
1 tbsp chia seeds
small pinch of salt
200g ground almonds
toasted almonds, to serve
blueberries, to serve

For the filling

120g ground almonds
1 tsp ground cinnamon
150g honey
3 eggs
125g coconut oil or butter
1 vanilla pod
200g blueberries

Preheat the oven to 160°C/325°F/gas mark 3.

To make the crust, blend the coconut oil, maple syrup, vanilla extract, chia seeds and salt in the food processor, then slowly fold in the ground almonds.

Grease a 26cm pie dish with some oil, then tip the crust mixture into the dish and spread out evenly. Using a fork, prick the pastry base. Cook in the oven for 12–15 minutes until golden.

While the crust is cooking, make the filling. Blend the ground almonds, cinnamon, honey, eggs and coconut oil in the blender. Scrape out the seeds from the vanilla pod and stir in along with the blueberries. Once the base is ready, remove from the oven and pour in the filling.

Bake for a further 30 minutes. Serve with a sprinkling of toasted almonds and some fresh berries.

Three-Ingredient Peaches and Cream Popsicles V GF DF

Another delicious summer fruit, the peach tastes amazing with cream. If you're looking for a really cooling dessert, it has to be my peaches and cream popsicles. They're a brilliant alcohol-free digestif – thanks to the dietary fibre in peaches and the yogurt – and a real crowd-pleaser. The perfect end to a summer BBQ.

Makes 8 popsicles

4 ripe peaches, stoned
   and quartered
2 tbsp honey
300g coconut yogurt
   or Greek yogurt

Put the peaches in a blender with 1 tablespoon of the honey and whizz until smooth. Separately blend the yogurt with the other tablespoon of honey.

Have 8 popsicle containers at the ready. Pour a quarter of the peach mixture across the 8 popsicle containers, then a quarter of the yogurt mixture. Continue to layer the peach and yogurt mixtures three more times. Put in lolly sticks and freeze overnight, or for 6 hours.

Once you are ready to eat them, run the moulds under hot water for 10 seconds to loosen the grip and you can pop out your popsicles.

These popsicles keep for 2–4 weeks in the freezer.

Raw Chocolate Peanut Butter Brownie Bites V GF DF PP 30

Energy balls are a staple in my house, but these feel like pure indulgence. Peanuts are a good source of protein if you're a gym bunny, but I also like to munch on one with a cup of refreshing peppermint tea in the garden.

Makes 14

150g peanut butter
75g hazelnuts or
  other nuts
200g Medjool dates, pitted
2 tbsp coconut oil
3 tbsp raw cacao powder
½ tsp ground cinnamon
pinch of salt

Place all the ingredients in a food processor and blitz until fully combined. Take a tablespoon of the mixture and roll between your hands into a ball. Place on a baking paper-lined tray. Repeat with the rest of the mixture, then pop the tray into the freezer for 30 minutes to set. Remove and put the brownie bites in the fridge, ready to enjoy.

The brownies will keep in the fridge for 2 weeks.

Autumn

Breakfast

Black Rice Porridge with Berries and Caramelised Banana

Three-Ingredient Banana Pancakes

Cashew Loaf

Four Autumn Ways on Toast: Avocado and Halloumi with Toasted Sesame Seeds, Sautéed Mushrooms and Smoked Paprika, Fig and Goat's Cheese, Almond Butter and Banana

Lean and Green Courgette Omelette

Soups, Salads and Snacks

Four Autum Side Salads: Ginger Spiced Cucumber Ribbons, Steamed Green Beans with Toasted Hazelnuts, Rocket and Caramelised Shallots, Grated Courgette Salad

Gracious Bowl

My Favourite Kale Salad

Torn Chicken Salad

Pumpkin and Red Cabbage Salad with Miso Dressing

Roasted Beetroot and Lentil Salad

Two Autumn Lunch Boxes: Middle Eastern Quinoa Chicken Pot, Buckwheat Noodle Salad with Broccoli and Pak Choi

Two Autumn Take-to-Work Snacks: Four-Ingredient Granola Bars, Peanut Butter Toffee Popcorn

Beetroot and Fennel Soup

Squash and Sweetcorn Soup

Mains

Sweet Potato and Broccoli Cakes

Carrot, Pea and Coconut Curry

Baked Sea Bream and Lentil Parcels with Green Goddess Pesto

Chicken Ramen

Cumin Roasted Aubergine Stuffed with Quinoa Tabbouleh

Chickpea and Aubergine Curry

Coconut Spiced Prawn Korma

Squash and Tomato Coconut Curry

Coconut and Pine Nut Pilau

Quick Tamari Spiced Mince

Dessert

Mini Crumbles

Chocolate Beet Cake

Plum and Almond Cake

Upside-Down Banana Cake

Black Rice Porridge
with Berries and Caramelised Banana

V GF DF 30

Blackberries are an autumn superfood. I've got memories from my childhood of going out blackberry picking with my mum, and returning home with berry-stained hands and juice all around my mouth. Blackberries contain bioflavonoids and vitamin C, which protects against sun damage and ageing.

Serves 1–2

100g black rice

400ml rice or almond milk, plus extra for topping

pinch of salt

1 tsp vanilla extract

1 tbsp maple syrup or honey

1 tbsp coconut oil

2 tbsp coconut sugar

1 banana, sliced in half lengthways

50g blackberries

50g blueberries

2 tbsp toasted coconut flakes

Rinse the rice and put into a pot along with the milk, 100ml of water and the salt. Bring to the boil, then let it simmer for 30 minutes until the rice has soaked up all the liquid. Turn off the heat and stir in the vanilla and maple syrup.

While the rice is cooking, heat the coconut oil in a small frying pan over a medium–high heat. Put half the coconut sugar into the pan and stir to dissolve, then add the banana halves. Cook for 2 minutes on each side until the banana is nice and caramelised.

Top the rice porridge with the caramelised banana halves, then the blackberries, blueberries and toasted coconut. Sprinkle over the remaining tablespoon of coconut sugar and pour on extra milk if you like.

Three-Ingredient Banana Pancakes Ⓥ ⒼⒻ Ⓓ ⓅⓅ ⑮

I often make banana pancakes with Kieran at the weekend after we've been to the gym together. Bananas are a great pre- or post- workout snack because they give you a quick burst of energy, and they replenish the potassium lost from sweating during your workout session, helping to maintain muscle and nerve function. Add some protein powder to supercharge these pancakes.

Makes 3 pancakes, serves 1

1 egg
1 banana
4 tbsp oats or
    protein powder
3 tbsp coconut oil

Toppings

melted good-quality
    dark chocolate
fresh berries, chopped
natural yogurt
maple syrup

Whisk the egg in a bowl and mash the banana into it. Add the oats and stir well. The mixture should be thicker than a crêpe batter but thinner than batter for a cake.

Heat the coconut oil in a small frying pan over a medium heat. Wait until the pan is hot, then spoon in 2 tablespoons of the mixture. Fry the pancake for 2 minutes on one side, then turn over and fry for a further minute or so, until cooked through. Repeat with the rest of the mixture.

To serve the pancakes, drizzle over melted dark chocolate and top with berries, yogurt and maple syrup.

Cashew Loaf

V GF PP

As the long summer days seem distant and the cold creeps in, it's so important to boost your immune system. Most of us think of increasing our vitamin C levels to do this, but we also need to focus on good gut health, as it's a key player in immune health. This probiotic-charged bread is perfect for boosting your gut bacteria, thanks to the natural yogurt.

Makes 1 medium loaf

450g raw cashews
½ tsp baking powder
¼ tsp gluten-free
   bicarbonate of soda
pinch of salt
3 large eggs, separated
125g natural yogurt
125ml apple juice or the
   fresh juice of 1 apple
coconut oil or butter,
   for greasing

Preheat your oven to 150°C/300°F/gas mark 2.

Place the cashews in a food processor and grind into a flour. Add the baking powder, bicarbonate of soda, salt, egg yolks, yogurt and apple juice. Process until smooth.

Tip the egg whites into a large mixing bowl and beat until they form stiff peaks. Gently fold the beaten egg whites into the cashew mixture. Grease a small loaf tin with oil and pour in the mixture.

Bake in the oven for 70 minutes until a knife inserted into the loaf comes out clean. Remove the loaf from the tin and leave to cool on a wire rack, then slice.

Toasted slices of this loaf go really well with almond butter and chopped banana (see page 147), poached eggs and salmon, mashed avocado with chilli, or bacon and roasted mushrooms.

Four Autumn Ways on Toast

Keeping a good variety of foods in your diet means you get a good range of nutrients, and it also means you never get bored. A few of these gorgeous recipes can be enjoyed all year round, but I particularly like figs when they come into season. They're bursting with dietary fibre, so they're good for the gut, and can be paired with both sweet and savoury dishes.

I always have some rye bread in the freezer ready for a toasty breakfast.

Serves 1

60g halloumi

1 tsp honey or
   maple syrup

1 tsp coconut oil

½ avocado, peeled
   and stoned

1 tsp toasted
   sesame seeds

salt, to taste

Avocado and Halloumi

with Toasted Sesame Seeds

(V) (D) 15

Cut the halloumi into 1cm slices and drizzle over the honey. Heat the coconut oil in a small frying pan over a medium heat and put the halloumi into the pan. Fry for a few minutes on each side until golden.

While the cheese is cooking, mash the avocado flesh. Spread on to your toast and sprinkle over some salt. Top with the pan-fried halloumi and the sesame seeds.

Serves 1

1 tsp avocado oil, coconut
   oil or butter

¼ tsp smoked paprika

¼ tsp dried oregano

100g mushrooms, sliced

salt and freshly ground
   black pepper, to taste

1 tsp toasted sunflower
   seeds

Sautéed Mushrooms and Smoked Paprika

 (V) DF (S) (D) 15

Heat the oil in a small frying pan with the smoked paprika and oregano. Add the mushrooms and a pinch of salt, then sauté for 5 minutes until the mushrooms shrink and are cooked through. Top your toast with the sautéed mushrooms, a grinding of salt and pepper and the sunflower seeds.

Serves 1

40g goat's cheese
1 tsp pesto
1 tsp olive oil
1 fig
2 walnuts, roughly
  chopped

Fig and Goat's Cheese

Spread the goat's cheese on to your toast. Stir the pesto together with the olive oil and drizzle over. Thinly slice the fig and place on top, then throw over the chopped walnuts. Dig in

Serves 1

2 tbsp almond butter
1 tsp cacao nibs
½ banana, sliced
1 tsp maple syrup

Almond Butter and Banana

Slather the almond butter on to your slice of toast. Top with the cacao nibs and banana slices, then drizzle over the maple syrup and enjoy.

Lean and Green Courgette Omelette

V GF DF S D PP 15

Courgettes and chillies come into season at the same time, which is awesome because they're the ultimate team. I love sneaking extra veggies into my food, and pairing courgette with egg makes this dish feel thick, decadent and filling – like a fritatta.

Serves 1

3 eggs
salt and freshly ground
  black pepper, to taste
½ courgette, grated
1 tbsp avocado oil
  or butter
½ avocado, peeled
  and stoned
½ lime, cut into wedges
¼ jalapeño chilli,
  deseeded and
  finely chopped
1 tbsp toasted almonds

Whisk the eggs with a pinch of salt and pepper. Squeeze the excess moisture from the grated courgette and add to the beaten eggs. Heat the oil in an omelette-sized frying pan. Wait until it's hot, then add the egg mixture and let it bubble for 30 seconds. Using a spatula, gently lift the sides of the omelette away from the edges of the pan, allowing the uncooked egg to run into the gaps. Cook for a few minutes more until just set, then turn off the heat.

Thinly slice the avocado flesh (squeeze on a little lime juice from one of your wedges so as not to brown) and place the avocado slices inside the omelette. Sprinkle with a pinch of salt, add the chopped jalapeño and toasted almonds, then fold the omelette over in half on top of the filling. Plate up with fresh lime wedges on the side.

Four Autumn Side Salads

Serves 2

1 cucumber
1 tsp sesame seeds

For the dressing

1 tsp freshly grated ginger
½ small shallot,
   finely chopped
1 tsp honey
1 tbsp lime juice
2 tbsp toasted
   sesame seeds
1 tsp tamari

Ginger Spiced Cucumber Ribbons V GF DF 15

Cucumber makes the most awesome salad ingredient. It's great to snack on, because it's got that satisfying crunch, it's juicy, and most of all it goes with sweet and salty Asian flavours! This is a brilliant dish to serve alongside duck or turkey, which are at their seasonal best in autumn. If you're a vegetarian, try serving alongside a stir-fry of wild mushrooms and toasted cashews for protein.

Whisk the dressing ingredients together. Peel the cucumber into ribbons and mix with the dressing. This goes well with Sweet Potato and Broccoli Cakes (see page 174) or the Baked Sea Bream and Lentil Parcels (see page 178).

Serves 4

400g green beans
50g toasted hazelnuts

For the dressing

½ shallot, finely chopped
4 tbsp extra virgin olive oil
3 tbsp sherry vinegar
2 tsp Dijon mustard
½ tsp salt
pinch of freshly ground
   black pepper

Steamed Green Beans
with Toasted Hazelnuts V GF DF S 15
VEGAN

This is an essential side dish – I can't have a meal without a side of something green. There's always something green in season at any time of the year, but in autumn there's nothing better than green beans for a boost of vitamin B, which allows the body to use and store energy from protein and carbohydrates in food.

Steam the beans over a pan of simmering water for 5 minutes, until just tender. While they're cooking, whisk together the dressing ingredients. Then drain the beans and toss them in the dressing. Top with the toasted hazelnuts.

Rocket and Caramelised Shallots Ⓥ GF DF 15

Serves 2

1 tsp coconut oil or butter
1 shallot, finely chopped
1 pear
lemon juice, for the pear
50g rocket

For the dressing

1 tbsp grainy mustard
1 tbsp balsamic vinegar
juice of ½ lemon
2 tbsp extra virgin olive oil
salt and freshly ground
    black pepper, to taste

Rocket is a great salad leaf. As well as its gorgeous peppery flavour, it contains lots of nutrients to boost your health and is a rich source of vitamins A, C and K.

Heat the oil in a small pan, then add the shallot and cook for 4–5 minutes until caramelised. Meanwhile, whisk the dressing ingredients together and thinly slice the pear (dipping the slices in a little lemon juice so as not to brown). Plate up the rocket, add the pear slices and caramelised shallot and then drizzle over the dressing.

Grated Courgette Salad Ⓥ GF DF 15

Serves 4

3 courgettes, grated
1 red chilli, deseeded and
    finely chopped

For the dressing

3 tbsp extra virgin olive oil
1 tbsp apple cider vinegar
1 tbsp honey
1 tsp freshly grated ginger
salt and freshly ground
    black pepper, to taste

This salad is a staple in my house, mainly because it's so easy to put together in a matter of minutes. Courgettes are a brilliant source of heart-healthy potassium and vitamin C, and the ginger and apple cider vinegar make this a great stomach-soothing salad that tastes amazing too!

Mix the dressing ingredients together with a pinch of salt and pepper. Then stir the dressing into the grated courgette and sprinkle over the red chilli before serving.

Gracious Bowl

V GF DF D PP 30

This gorgeous Gracious Bowl is full of my favourite autumnal veg. During the autumn, it's getting a bit chillier but we're still craving salad, so this dish is a great mix of raw veg and warm comfort food. Brightly coloured radishes and soothing fennel add an incredible crunch, quinoa gives us that protein our bodies need for our muscles, and topped off with eggs this is a total winner for breakfast, lunch or dinner.

Serves 2

2 tbsp coconut oil
    or butter
1 fennel bulb, thinly sliced
1 red onion, thinly sliced
salt and freshly ground
    black pepper, to taste
80g quinoa
50g pine nuts
50g radishes
1 apple, cored
juice of 1 lemon
2 tbsp olive oil
2 eggs

Heat 1 tablespoon of the coconut oil in a pan. Add the fennel and red onion, add a pinch of salt and pepper and sauté for 10–15 minutes until caramelised.

Meanwhile, rinse the quinoa in a sieve, and put in a pot with a pinch of salt. Pour over 250ml of water (to cover). Bring to the boil, then turn down the heat and let it simmer for 12–15 minutes, until the quinoa is cooked through and all the water has been absorbed.

Heat a small frying pan to a medium–high heat, add the pine nuts and toast for 2 minutes, shaking the pan to prevent them burning. Then let the pine nuts cool on a plate.

Thinly slice the radishes and apple, and cover in the lemon juice to avoid browning. Stir the caramelised fennel and onion mixture into the cooked quinoa, along with the sliced radishes and apple. Pour over the olive oil, add a large pinch of salt and the toasted pine nuts, and mix.

Just before serving, heat the remaining tablespoon of coconut oil in a fresh pan. Crack in the eggs and fry for a few minutes, or as desired. Top your salad with the fried eggs, sunny side up.

My Favourite Kale Salad

V GF DF S PP 15

Kale is king. It's super good for us, but also happens to make a great salad. Sometimes I massage my kale so that it goes soft, but during the autumn I like to sauté it so that it wilts and it's warm. The chickpeas are really filling, and the currants and nuts are an awesome energy-boosting ingredient – and we need that extra energy to keep our bodies warm!

Serves 2–3

1 tbsp coconut oil
200g kale, finely chopped
salt, to taste
400g can chickpeas,
    rinsed and drained
1 avocado
juice of 1 lemon
1 apple
50g currants or raisins
30g toasted flaked
    almonds

For the dressing

3 tbsp olive oil
2 tbsp maple syrup
1 tbsp vinegar
1 tsp grainy mustard
big pinch of salt and
    freshly ground black
    pepper

Get the dressing ready first by whisking all the dressing ingredients together in a cup or jug. Next, heat the coconut oil in a large frying pan over a medium–high heat and, once the oil is hot, add the kale and a pinch of salt. Sauté the kale for 3–4 minutes. Toss the still-warm kale with the dressing in a large bowl and leave to the side to cool.

Grab a quarter of the chickpeas and place them on a chopping board. Roughly chop so the chickpeas turn into chunks, then throw them in with the kale and mix well. Repeat with the rest of the chickpeas in batches. Peel and stone the avocado, then chop into chunks and squeeze over half the lemon juice so it doesn't brown. Core and grate the apple, then mix with the remaining lemon juice. Mix the currants, avocado and apple into the salad and top with the flaked almonds.

Torn Chicken Salad

GF DF PP I5

I'm a big fan of chicken salads because they're very quick and easy to make. When we don't have a lot of time on our hands, this salad is the perfect thing to whip up. It's got a brilliant oriental flavour, with ginger helping to fight against cold viruses brought on by a change in season. Make sure you use good-quality organic free-range chicken, and if you've never heard of tamari, it's just gluten-free soy sauce, so feel free to swap this out!

Serves 2

2 chicken breasts
salt and freshly ground
    black pepper, to taste
1 tbsp coconut oil
    or butter
200g green beans
200g sugar snap peas
200g mangetout
2 tbsp black sesame seeds
1 red chilli, deseeded
    and finely chopped
1 tbsp chopped fresh
    parsley
30g toasted hazelnuts

For the dressing

1 tsp freshly grated ginger
½ small shallot,
    finely chopped
1 tsp honey
1 tbsp lime juice
2 tbsp toasted sesame oil
1 tsp tamari

Rub the chicken breasts with a little salt and pepper. Heat the oil in a pan, add the chicken and fry for 6 minutes on each side until cooked through. Leave to cool for a few minutes, then shred.

Steam the green beans, sugar snaps and mangetout over a pot of simmering water for 2 minutes, then drain and place in ice-cold water.

Make the dressing by whisking together all the ingredients. Stir the blanched veg into the dressing, adding a pinch of salt and the black sesame seeds. Top the salad with the chilli and parsley, then with the shredded chicken and the hazelnuts. Serve immediately.

Pumpkin and Red Cabbage Salad

with Miso Dressing

V GF DF S PP

There's something so refreshing about a miso-dressed warm salad. Miso is really good for digestion because it's a fermented food, which promotes good bacteria in the gut. I love it all year round, but it goes particularly well with pumpkin and squashes, which we all know and love around October time.

Serves 4

1 pumpkin or large squash, peeled and deseeded

4 carrots

2 tbsp coconut oil or melted butter

salt, to taste

100g buckwheat

¼ red cabbage, cored and thinly sliced

100g kale, thinly sliced

1 cucumber

4 tbsp toasted sesame seeds, to serve

For the miso dressing

2 tbsp miso paste

3 tbsp brown rice vinegar

1 tbsp lemon juice

3 tbsp toasted sesame seeds

1 tbsp maple syrup

pinch of cayenne pepper

2 tbsp water

Preheat the oven to 200°C/400°F/gas mark 6.

Chop the pumpkin and carrots into 2½cm chunks and place in a large roasting tray. Pour over the oil and sprinkle with plenty of salt. Roast in the oven for 45–55 minutes until golden and cooked through.

While the veg is roasting, cook the buckwheat. Rinse the grains, then place in a large pot with a pinch of salt and 250ml of water. Bring to the boil and simmer for 12 minutes until the water is totally absorbed and the buckwheat has just softened. Turn off the heat and throw in the cabbage and kale, keeping the lid on to slightly steam the kale.

Whisk the dressing ingredients together. Cut the cucumber in half lengthways and slice into ½cm-thick semicircles. Mix the roasted veg, buckwheat and greens, and the cucumber all together. Pour on the dressing, stir it through and serve with the toasted sesame seeds sprinkled over.

Roasted Beetroot and Lentil Salad

(V) GF DF PP

When it comes to root veg season I jump for joy because it means the return of the awesome beetroot! Beets are really high in flavonoid antioxidants, which protect us from free radicals, and vitamin A, which is essential for vision. They're filling, tasty and go brilliantly with lentils for a satisfying side dish.

Serves 2

4 large beetroots
2 tbsp coconut oil
   or butter, melted
salt and freshly ground
   black pepper, to taste
1 red onion, chopped
2 garlic cloves, crushed
400g can lentils, rinsed
   and drained
sprig of fresh thyme, leaves
   picked and chopped, or
   ½ tsp dried thyme
grated zest of ¼ lemon
1 pear

For the dressing

2 tsp freshly grated ginger
1 tbsp olive oil
1 tbsp sesame oil
2 tbsp lemon juice
2 tsp Dijon mustard
pinch of salt

Preheat the oven to 180°C/350°F/gas mark 4.

Cut the beets into quarters, place in a roasting tray and rub in 1 tablespoon of the coconut oil and some salt and pepper. Roast the beets for 40 minutes until cooked through.

While the beets are in the oven, heat the other tablespoon of oil in a pan. Add the red onion and sauté for 7 minutes, until golden, then add the garlic and stir for a few minutes. Add the lentils, thyme, 1 tablespoon of water and the lemon zest to the pan and cook for 5 minutes, adding more water if it gets dry. Leave to cool.

Thinly slice the pear and stir into the lentil mixture. Whisk the dressing ingredients together and mix half in. Plate up and top with the roasted beetroots, then drizzle over the rest of the dressing to serve.

Two Autumn Lunch Boxes

When the days start getting colder you need something nourishing waiting for you at lunchtime. These delicious and simple lunch boxes will be the envy of your work colleagues!

Middle Eastern Quinoa Chicken Pot GF DF PP 15

Serves 1

50g cooked quinoa
1 chicken breast, cooked and shredded
1 carrot, grated
2 tbsp hummus
1 tsp sesame seeds

For the dressing

1 tbsp olive oil
1 tbsp tahini
½ tsp ground cumin
2 tbsp water
pinch of salt

Mix the quinoa, chicken and carrot together in your lunch container, dollop on the hummus and sprinkle over the seeds.

To make your dressing, whisk the ingredients together well in a small jar. Then take some kitchen foil and cut out a hand-sized square. Make a small 'bowl' dent in the middle of the foil with your thumb and carefully pour the dressing into it, then wrap it up tight. Pop the foil dressing package on top of your salad, ready to dress when it comes to lunchtime.

Buckwheat Noodle Salad  V GF DF S 15
with Broccoli and Pak Choi

Serves 1

2 tsp tamari
1 tsp freshly grated ginger
1 garlic clove, crushed
1 tbsp sesame oil
60g cooked buckwheat noodles
½ broccoli head, chopped
1 pak choi, ends sliced off
1 red chilli, deseeded and finely chopped
20g toasted cashews

Whisk the tamari, ginger, garlic and sesame oil together. Then toss in the buckwheat noodles and place in your lunch box.

Steam the broccoli over a pan of simmering water for 4 minutes until cooked through, adding the pak choi for the last 30 seconds to lightly steam. Drain the veg, then leave to cool before mixing with the noodles. Top with the cashews. Keep in the fridge until lunchtime.

Two Autumn Take-to-Work Snacks

Popcorn isn't just for the movies! Stick this delicious and easy-to-make popcorn in a little tub with a light, super easy grab-and-go granola bar to make 4pm your favourite time of the day.

Makes 6–8 bars

25g coconut oil, melted and cooled, plus extra for greasing
120g rolled oats
85g maple syrup or honey
45g peanut butter or almond butter

Four-Ingredient Granola Bars

V DF PP

Grease a baking tray with a little coconut oil. Put the oats in a bowl and pour over all the other ingredients. Mix together well. Press the mixture into the baking tray and flatten with a spatula. Leave to cool in the fridge for an hour or two until it hardens. Slice into bars, then keep in the fridge until you want to eat them.

3 tbsp coconut oil
40g popping corn
1 tbsp peanut butter
salt, to taste
2 tbsp date syrup

Peanut Butter Toffee Popcorn

V GF DF 15

Put the oil in a large pot over a medium heat and leave to heat up. Put the popping corn, peanut butter and a pinch of salt into the pot. Stir well, then place the lid on.

After a minute the corn will start to pop! Keep the pot over the heat for 2–3 minutes and wait for the popping to slow down or stop. Then take off the heat, carefully remove the lid and pour over the date syrup. Stir the syrup through, then tip out on to a baking paper-lined tray. Leave the nutty toffee popcorn to cool.

Beetroot and Fennel Soup

(V) GF DF

I love a soup in the autumn, it's the perfect time for it when root vegetables are in their element. You'll often find me curled up on the couch with a big bowl of this on a cold day. This beetroot soup has the most amazing colour, and is rich and creamy thanks to the coconut. Warm yourself right up with this number.

Serves 4

2 tbsp coconut oil
   or butter

4 shallots, finely chopped

salt and freshly ground
   black pepper, to taste

4 garlic cloves, crushed

500g beetroot, peeled
   and chopped into
   chunks

2 fennel bulbs, chopped
   into chunks

400g can coconut milk

500ml veggie or
   chicken stock

2 tbsp chopped fresh dill

Heat the oil in a pan, add the shallots and a pinch of salt, and sauté for 5 minutes. Add the garlic and stir for a minute, then add the chopped beetroot, fennel and another pinch of salt. Stir for 30 seconds, then pour over the coconut milk and stock. Bring to a simmer and cook for 40 minutes. Blend the soup until smooth, season, and top with the chopped dill to serve.

Squash and Sweetcorn Soup

V GF DF

Squash and sweetcorn is a winning combo. Cooked down with a bit of spice from the smoked paprika and topped with some salty olives, it's the perfect thing to make a batch of and savour on a dreamy autumnal evening.

Serves 4

2 corn on the cob ears

2 tbsp coconut oil
or butter

1 white onion, finely
chopped

2 garlic cloves, crushed

1 tsp smoked paprika

salt, to taste

1 large squash, approx.
1kg, peeled and
chopped into chunks

500ml veggie or
chicken stock

juice of ½ lemon

2 tbsp chopped
fresh parsley

2 tbsp chopped olives

Cut the corn kernels from the corn on the cob. Heat the oil in a large pot, add the onion and sauté for 5 minutes. Add the garlic, smoked paprika and a big pinch of salt and cook for another minute. Next add the squash, corn kernels and a pinch of salt, and stir well for 30 seconds. Pour over the stock and lemon juice, bring to simmering point and simmer for 40 minutes. Blend the soup until smooth. Season and stir in the parsley, then serve with the chopped olives sprinkled on top.

Sweet Potato and Broccoli Cakes

(V) (DF)

I love this recipe because I always find I have leftover sweet potatoes and broccoli in my fridge at the end of the week. So in an effort to minimise waste, one evening I invented these sweet potato and broccoli cakes and was pleasantly surprised. They're awesome for sneaking veg into food, so if you have fussy kids then these are a winner.

Makes 4 cakes, serves 2

2 large sweet potatoes (about 300g)

1 broccoli head

2 tbsp coconut oil or butter, plus extra for brushing

2 spring onions, finely chopped

2 tsp ground cumin

1 tsp ground coriander

½ tsp turmeric

salt, to taste

3 tbsp porridge oats

½ tsp dried chilli flakes

1 tbsp sesame seeds

Preheat the oven to 190°C/375°F/gas mark 5.

Chop the sweet potatoes into small chunks and steam over a pan of simmering water for 10 minutes, then drain. While this is cooking, chop the broccoli into little florets. Heat the oil in a pan and add the florets. Add the spring onions, cumin, coriander, turmeric and a big pinch of salt to the broccoli. Sauté for 5 minutes, then leave to one side.

Place the cooked sweet potato and broccoli in a large bowl and mash together. Add the oats, another big pinch of salt and the chilli flakes, and mix well. Using your hands, roll into 4 evenly sized patties. Place them on a baking tray lined with baking paper. Brush with a little oil and coat in the sesame seeds.

Bake in the oven for 20–25 minutes until golden and crispy. Delicious served with a green salad.

Carrot, Pea and Coconut Curry

V GF DF 30

Curry is a British staple 365 days a year, and it's so versatile. You can create so many combinations and flavours, depending on the season. Here I'm taking advantage of gorgeous carrots, which are brilliant in a curry because of their natural sweetness. An old wives' tale says that they also help you see in the dark, which is perfect for when the days get shorter and nights get longer!

Serves 2

1 tbsp coconut oil
1 red onion, chopped
salt, to taste
1 tsp mustard seeds
1 tsp ground cumin
1 tbsp freshly grated ginger
1 red chilli, chopped
4 large carrots, chopped
400ml can coconut milk
1 tsp turmeric
200g frozen peas
1 tsp garam masala
1 tbsp chopped fresh
   coriander

Heat the oil in a large pan, add the onion and a pinch of salt, and cook for 5 minutes. Add the mustard seeds and stir until they start to pop, then add the cumin, ginger, chilli and carrots and stir well. Pour over the coconut milk and add the turmeric, plus another pinch of salt. Turn down the heat and simmer for 20 minutes. Stir in the peas and warm them through. Just before serving, add the garam masala and stir well. Serve with the fresh coriander sprinkled on top.

This goes really well with a side of cauliflower rice.

Baked Sea Bream and Lentil Parcels

GF S D PP 15

with Green Goddess Pesto

Many people tend to stick with more popular fish like salmon and cod, but there are so many tasty, nutritious types of fish and the less popular ones tend to be a little more friendly on your pocket too. I love sea bream because it tastes delicious with green pesto. Serve this with some sweet potato wedges for an extra-nutritious take on fish and chips!

Serves 2

2 sea bream or
   sea bass fillets
salt, to taste
400g can lentils,
   rinsed and drained
lemon wedges, to serve

**For the green
goddess pesto**

25g fresh basil leaves
10g fresh mint leaves
50g roasted pistachios
½ jalapeño chilli,
   deseeded and roughly
   chopped
100ml olive oil
juice of 1 lemon
½ tsp salt
2 tbsp shaved Parmesan
   or nutritional yeast

Preheat the oven to 200°C/400°F/gas mark 6.

Blend the pesto ingredients together in a food processor. Sprinkle plenty of salt on to the fish fillets.

Cut out two 30cm squares of baking paper and place on a roasting tray. Carefully put half the lentils in the middle of one paper square and half in the other. Spoon 2 tablespoons of pesto on to each pile of lentils. Place the sea bream on top and then spoon another tablespoon of pesto on top of each fillet. Pick up the baking paper corners and wrap the fish parcels up, twisting to secure.

Bake in the oven for 10 minutes until just cooked through. Squeeze over fresh lemon juice and serve.

Any leftover pesto can be kept in the fridge for 5–7 days.

Chicken Ramen

GF DF D PP 30

This is my take on one of our Japanese favourites. Ramen has totally exploded in popularity in recent years, but what many people don't realise is that it's so easy to make at home when you want a warming meal. Chicken stock is great when you're feeling run-down because it contains immune-boosting minerals such as calcium, magnesium, phosphorus, silicon and sulphur, which makes ramen such fantastic comfort food.

Serves 2

1 tbsp coconut oil
  or butter
1 tsp freshly grated ginger
1 garlic clove, crushed
500ml chicken stock
200g button mushrooms
1 red chilli, deseeded
  and finely chopped
1 tbsp tamari or soy sauce
2 chicken breasts or
  thighs, cut into strips
100g rice noodles
2 eggs
salt, to taste
2 carrots, julienned
juice of ½ lime
2 spring onions,
  finely chopped
1 tbsp toasted
  sesame seeds

Heat the oil in a large pan, add the ginger and garlic and sauté for 30 seconds. Next add the stock, mushrooms, chilli, tamari and chicken pieces. Cook for 20 minutes.

Meanwhile, cook your rice noodles as per the packet instructions in a separate pot. In another pot, boil the eggs in plenty of water for 4 minutes, until the whites are cooked but the yolk is still runny. Once cool enough to handle, peel and slice the eggs in half and sprinkle on a little salt.

Just before serving, throw the carrots and cooked noodles into the soup and squeeze in the lime juice. Top with the boiled egg halves, spring onions and sesame seeds, then serve immediately.

Cumin Roasted Aubergine

V GF DF PP

Stuffed with Quinoa Tabbouleh

Roasted aubergine is an absolute dream for a veggie-based meal. I love Middle Eastern-inspired flavours because the spices really bring heat to the dish. The smoky aubergine feels filling and meaty, and you're getting a tasty bit of protein from the quinoa.

Serves 2

2 large aubergines

4 tbsp coconut oil
or melted butter

1 tbsp ground cumin

2 tsp ground coriander

¼ tsp turmeric

1 tsp chilli powder

1 green chilli, deseeded
and finely chopped

salt, to taste

For the quinoa tabbouleh

100g quinoa

2 tbsp chopped
fresh parsley

juice of ½ lemon

1 tbsp olive oil

1 beef tomato, diced

salt, to taste

Preheat the oven to 200°C/400°F/gas mark 6.

Slice the aubergines in half and score them on the inside. Rub in the coconut oil, spices, green chilli and salt. Place the aubergine halves on a roasting tray and put in the oven. Roast for 45–50 minutes until completely softened. You want the texture to melt in your mouth.

Meanwhile, rinse the quinoa in a sieve and place in a pot with 250ml of water. Bring to a boil, then turn it down to a simmer and cook for 12 minutes, until cooked through and the water has been absorbed. Mix the quinoa with the parsley, lemon juice, olive oil, tomato and a good pinch of salt.

Take the aubergines out of the oven and top with the quinoa tabbouleh. Serve and enjoy.

Chickpea and Aubergine Curry

(V) GF DF PP 30

Chickpeas are a great source of veggie protein, and mixed with aubergine you've got a really fragrant textured curry. Chickpeas are a great source of vitamins B1 and B6, which help the body to produce energy (which you'll definitely need when it gets colder) and red blood cells.

Serves 2–3

2 tbsp coconut oil
 or butter

2 garlic cloves, crushed

1 tsp freshly grated ginger

1 tbsp red Thai curry paste

1 red pepper, deseeded
 and thinly sliced

1 aubergine, cut into
 2cm cubes

pinch of salt

400g can chickpeas

1 tbsp tamari

400ml can coconut milk

1 tbsp chopped fresh basil

1 lime, cut into wedges

Heat the oil in a large pan. Add the garlic, ginger and red Thai curry paste, stir and cook for 30 seconds. Then add the pepper strips, aubergine pieces and 2 tablespoons of water. Coat the veggies in the spices and add the salt. Stir for another minute, then add the chickpeas and tamari, and pour over the coconut milk. Stir again, turn down the heat and simmer for 30 minutes until the aubergine is cooked through. Serve hot with a squeeze of fresh lime juice.

Coconut Spiced Prawn Korma

GF DF PP 15

Prawns are one of my favourite seafoods because they taste really meaty, making them great in a curry. They're high in protein, and in flavour! There's a common misconception that making curry is difficult because it takes time to put all of the spices together – so we opt for convenient pre-made sauces which can be full of nasties. This is my all-time favourite korma recipe, which tastes better than any takeaway you'll have.

Serves 2

50g cashews
400ml can coconut milk
2 tbsp avocado oil
½ tsp cumin seeds
1 white onion, finely chopped
pinch of salt
2 garlic cloves, crushed
1 tsp ground coriander
1 tsp paprika
⅓ tsp turmeric
½ tsp garam masala
¼ tsp ground cardamom
1 large beef tomato, chopped
1 red chilli, chopped
300g raw prawns, shelled

Whizz the cashews and coconut milk together in a blender until smooth.

Heat the oil in a large pot over a medium heat, throw in the cumin seeds and let them start to become fragrant for a moment. Turn down the heat to medium, add the onion and salt and sauté for 4 minutes.

Add the garlic, coriander, paprika, turmeric, garam masala and ground cardamom to the onion, stir well to coat in the oil, then add the tomato and fresh chilli. Stir and cook for a few more minutes, then pour over the coconut and cashew mixture.

Leave the curry to cook for 5 minutes in the nutty coconut milk, then add the prawns. Cook for a further 3 minutes until the prawns turn pink. Serve with cauliflower rice or brown rice.

Squash and Tomato Coconut Curry

V GF DF

Squash season is one of my favourites. Our bodies crave root vegetables as it gets colder because they are warming and easily digestible. I love adding coconut milk to my curries because it contains medium-chain fatty acids, one of which is lauric acid. Lauric acid is converted in the body to an antiviral and antibacterial compound called monolaurin, which is known to destroy a variety of disease-causing organisms, including colds!

Serves 2–3

1 lemongrass stalk

1 tbsp coconut oil
   or butter

1 tbsp freshly grated ginger

2 garlic cloves, crushed

1 red chilli, finely chopped

4 spring onions, chopped

1 large butternut squash,
   peeled and cut into
   cubes

500g beef tomatoes,
   chopped

salt, to taste

400ml can coconut milk

½ tsp turmeric

2 courgettes, grated

juice of 1 lime

200g frozen peas

2 tbsp chopped fresh
   coriander

Using the back of a spoon, peel off the outer layer from the lemongrass, then roughly chop. Pop into a food processor with 1–2 tablespoons of water and blitz into a paste. Add more water if necessary.

Heat the oil in a large pan and add the lemongrass paste, ginger, garlic, chilli and spring onions. Sauté for a few minutes, then add the squash and tomatoes and cook for another 2 minutes, adding a pinch of salt. Pour over the coconut milk and add the turmeric, courgettes and another pinch of salt. Turn down the heat and simmer for 30 minutes, until the squash is cooked through.

Just before serving, add the lime juice, frozen peas and coriander, and stir well until the peas are warmed through. Serve with brown rice or cauliflower rice.

Coconut and Pine Nut Pilau

(V) GF DF (S) PP 30

A deliciously fragrant side dish, this is great for a family meal or dinner party. It's gorgeously spiced, which mixes things up from just plain rice! I love adding pomegranate seeds to rice for a sweet crunch. As well as being really tasty, they also happen to be really good for you – rich in fibre, vitamins, minerals and bioactive plant compounds.

Serves 4

60ml coconut oil,
    avocado oil or butter
1 onion, chopped
1 garlic clove, crushed
1 tsp ground allspice
1 tsp ground cumin
300g basmati rice
500ml veggie stock
50g toasted desiccated
    coconut
50g toasted pine nuts
seeds from 1 pomegranate,
    or 200g seeds
2 figs, sliced

Heat the oil in a large pot over a medium heat. Add the onion and sauté for 3 minutes, then add the garlic and spices. Stir and cook for another minute. Add the rice to the pot, coat well in the oil and spices, then pour in the stock. Simmer for 15 minutes, then turn off the heat and leave to stand for 5 minutes. Fluff up the rice and serve, topped with the desiccated coconut, pine nuts, pomegranate seeds and sliced figs.

Quick Tamari Spiced Mince

GF DF PP 15

Looking for a quick dinner? Then this will be a go-to dish. As my parents are from New Zealand, lamb is a staple in my diet. It's really high in zinc and iron, which the body finds easier to absorb from lamb than from other sources. Zinc is incredible for the immune system and helps banish acne. Just make sure you buy grass-fed organic.

Serves 2–3

1 tbsp coconut oil
  or butter
500g lamb mince
3 tbsp tamari
1 tbsp freshly grated ginger
3 garlic cloves, crushed
1 lemongrass stalk,
  grated (optional)
2 beef tomatoes, chopped
1 courgette, grated
1 tbsp chopped fresh basil

Heat the oil in a large frying pan. Put the mince and 2 tablespoons of the tamari into the pan and brown for a few minutes. Add the ginger, garlic and lemongrass (if using) then cook for a further minute or two. Next, add the tomatoes, courgette and the remaining tablespoon of tamari and cook for another 5 minutes until the tomatoes have softened into a sauce. Serve topped with the chopped basil.

This goes well with the side salads on pages 152–153.

Mini Crumbles

V DF

The humble crumble is a British favourite. It's the ultimate way to top off a meal, but it definitely doesn't have to be full of refined sugar. Apples are the perfect sweet treat, bursting with fibre and brilliant for digestion. Whip up these mini crumbles after a roast!

Serves 4

2 tbsp coconut oil
  or butter, plus extra
  for greasing
2 cooking apples
2 tsp ground cinnamon
4 tbsp coconut sugar
  or honey
1 cardamom pod
70g porridge oats
pinch of salt

Preheat the oven to 170°C/325°F/gas mark 3.

Heat 1 tablespoon of the oil in a frying pan. Peel, core and slice the apples into chunks and put into the pan. Cook on a low heat for a few minutes, stirring regularly. Add 1 teaspoon of the cinnamon, 2 tablespoons of the sugar and the cardamom pod. Stir and leave to cook for 10 minutes, until the apple has softened. Remove the cardamom pod if you can find it. Using a spatula, scrape the cooked apple mixture into 4 small ramekins greased with butter or coconut oil.

Put the remaining tablespoon of oil into the same pan to melt, then take it off the heat. Stir in the oats, the remaining 2 tablespoons of sugar, the remaining teaspoon of cinnamon and the salt. Stir well until fully combined. Scrape this crumble mixture on top of the apples in the ramekins, using the spatula again. Pop into the oven to bake for 20–25 minutes.

Serve with yogurt or cream.

Chocolate Beet Cake

V GF DF S D PP 30

Root veggies are the best, and the mighty beet goes really well with chocolate due to its sweeter taste. Hide it in a chocolate cake and it makes the flavour beautifully rich, sweet and fudgy. A real treat for the tastebuds!

Serves 12

200g good-quality dark chocolate (I love Ombar)
125g coconut oil or butter, plus extra for greasing
125g coconut sugar
1 vanilla pod
4 eggs
2 beetroots (approx. 100g), grated
200g ground almonds
pinch of salt
handful of goji berries

Preheat your oven to 180°C/350°F/gas mark 4.

Break the chocolate into pieces. Carefully melt in a heatproof bowl over a pot of simmering water on a low heat. Then leave to one side.

Place the coconut oil and sugar in a food processor and cream together for a few minutes. Cut the vanilla pod in half and scrape out the vanilla seeds. Separate the eggs into yolks and whites. Pour the yolks into the food processor, along with the grated beets, melted chocolate, ground almonds, vanilla seeds and salt. Process until well combined and pour the mixture into a large bowl.

Whisk the egg whites until fluffy. Fold the whites into the chocolate mixture and stir gently.

Grease a 21cm cake tin with coconut oil. Pour in the cake batter, then pop into the oven. Bake for 20 minutes, then remove and leave to cool in the tin for 10 minutes. Decorate with goji berries.

Plum and Almond Cake

(V) (GF) (DF) (D)

Plums are the ultimate autumnal fruit (sorry figs!). Plump and juicy, they can spice up any porridge or pudding with the chop of a knife. Almonds and plums go really well together, and this cake is perfect for teatime with your mum or your friends!

Serves 12

175g coconut oil or butter, plus extra for greasing

175g coconut sugar

3 eggs

grated zest of 1 orange

300g ground almonds

1 tsp gluten-free baking powder

½ tsp bicarbonate of soda

1 vanilla pod, seeds scraped out

300g plums

2 tbsp toasted desiccated coconut, to serve

Preheat the oven to 170°C/325°F/gas mark 3.

Cream the coconut oil and sugar together in a food processor. Add the eggs one by one, mixing well each time, and stir in the orange zest. In a bowl, mix the ground almonds, baking powder, bicarb and vanilla seeds together. Then pour this into the wet mixture and process.

Stone the plums and slice into eighths.

Grease a 24cm cake tin. Pour in a third of the batter, then place a third of the plums on top. Repeat again with another third of the cake mixture and a third of the plums. Finally, pour in the rest of the cake mixture followed by the last of the plums. Bake in the oven for 60 minutes until cooked through and a knife inserted into the cake comes out clean.

Sprinkle over the toasted coconut while the cake is still warm, and serve.

This keeps for 3 days in an airtight container and goes really well with yogurt and a grating of chocolate.

Upside-Down Banana Cake

V GF DF D

Banana cake is a childhood favourite. I remember my mum making it with the over-ripe bananas from the fruit bowl, and me and my brother and sister munching on a hot slice straight from the oven. You probably know that bananas are a great source of quick-release energy, which makes this cake perfect if you're feeling a bit drained. I have even been known to munch on it pre-gym for a speedy slice of energy!

Serves 12

150g coconut oil or butter,
  plus extra for greasing
150g honey or date syrup
4 bananas
170g coconut sugar
grated zest and juice
  of 1 lime
½ tsp baking powder
1 tsp ground cinnamon
3 eggs
150g ground almonds

Preheat the oven to 170°C/325°F/gas mark 3 and grease a 20cm pie tin with oil.

Blend 25g of the oil with 125g of the honey, and spread over the base of the tin. Slice the bananas and spread evenly in a layer on top.

Cream the coconut sugar with the remaining 125g of oil and 25g of honey in a food processor until smooth. Add the lime zest, baking powder and cinnamon, and stir well. Add the eggs, one at a time, mixing well, then slowly add the ground almonds and stir through the lime juice. Spread the batter over the bananas. Press down with a spoon or spatula to make it flat.

Bake for 50 minutes in the oven. Remove and allow to cool, then flip the cake over to serve.

Winter

Breakfast

Quinoa Pancakes with Blood Orange Slices

Wilted Spinach, Feta and Dukka Omelette

Gym Bunny Smoothie

Four Porridges: Poached Pear, Cacao Nib and Almond Butter, Clementine, Chocolate and Toasted Hazelnut, Apple Pie

Soups, Salads and Snacks

Four Winter Side Dishes: Steamed Kale with Honey Mustard Dressing, Crispy Parsnip Fries, Clementine and Chicory Salad, Roasted Celeriac Wedges

Butter Bean and Cauliflower Soup

Immunity-Proof Chicken and Ginger Soup

Kale and Fennel Salad with a Chilli Lime Dressing

Buckwheat and Kale Salad with Radishes, Pomegranate and Balsamic Dressing

Two Winter Lunch Boxes: Smoked Mackerel and Beetroot Pot, Sweet Potato and Coconut Slaw

Two Winter Take-to-Work Snacks: Miso Soup, Sweet Potato Dip with Crudités

Mains

Basmati Rice Bowl with Crispy Brussels

Chicken Breast with Spiced Carrots and Cauliflower Tabbouleh

Indian Spiced Vegetable Curry

Oregano and Thyme Spiced Beef Stew

Red Rice and Roasted Leeks Chimichurri Bowl

Quinoa and Maple-Roasted Squash Bowl

Cashew and Chickpea Chicken Curry

Spicy Bean Stew

My Favourite Dhal Recipe

Slow-Roast Lamb Shoulder with Celeriac Mash and Greens

Pan-Fried Steak with Sweet Potato Mash, Toasted Mustard Seeds and Shallot Sauce

Dessert

Raw Peanut Butter Bars

Easy-Peasy Coconut Cookies

Lemon Drizzle Cake

Quinoa Pancakes
with Blood Orange Slices

V DF D 15

Blood oranges, like regular oranges, are full of vitamin C, which is a powerful antioxidant that helps keep gums healthy, repairs tissue and heals wounds. This picture-perfect fruit tastes awesome with coconut, and served alongside pancakes, this dish makes the ultimate weekend Instagram-worthy breakfast!

Makes 6 pancakes, serves 2

2 blood oranges
2 tbsp coconut oil
  or butter
1 tbsp maple syrup, plus
  extra to serve
75g desiccated coconut

For the pancake batter

240ml almond milk
1 egg
2 tsp vanilla extract
90g cooked quinoa
60g spelt flour
2 tbsp coconut sugar
½ tsp salt

Blend the pancake batter ingredients together in a food processor or blender and leave to the side to rest.

Slice the oranges into 1cm-thick rounds, leaving the peel still on. Heat 1 tablespoon of the coconut oil and the maple syrup in a pan over a medium–high heat. Fry the orange slices for 2 minutes on each side, then remove from the heat and leave to the side.

Take another pan and heat the remaining tablespoon of coconut oil. Let the oil get hot, then spoon in 2 tablespoons of the pancake batter. Fry the pancake for 2 minutes on each side until cooked through. Repeat with the rest of the batter, keeping the finished pancakes warm on the side.

Serve the pancakes with the jammy blood orange slices, an extra drizzle of maple syrup and a sprinkle of desiccated coconut.

Wilted Spinach, Feta and Dukkah Omelette

V GF S D PP 15

Eggs are one of my favourite brekkie options. They're cheap, easy to prepare and taste great! Loaded with choline, a brain-boosting nutrient, they also contain high-quality protein and healthy fats. Whenever I eat eggs for breakfast they always keep me going until lunchtime. I like to add different flavours to my eggs, and this Middle Eastern-inspired omelette will take no time at all to whip up in the morning.

Serves 1

3 eggs

salt and freshly ground
  black pepper, to taste

50g feta, crumbled

1 tsp dukkah

1 tbsp coconut oil
  or butter

1 garlic clove, crushed

50g spinach

Whisk the eggs together in a bowl with a pinch of salt and pepper. Mix the feta with the dukkah. Heat the coconut oil in a pan, then add the garlic and stir for 15 seconds. Add the spinach and a pinch of salt, and sauté for a minute or two, until the spinach wilts. Pour over the beaten eggs. Cook for a few minutes until the egg is no longer runny. Use a spatula to lift the edges so that the uncooked egg can seep to the bottom. Sprinkle the feta mix over one half of the omelette, then fold the other half over on top. Serve while still hot.

Gym Bunny Smoothie

V GF DF S 15

Need a quick smoothie on the go pre- or post-gym? This is one of my favourites. I like to add protein powder as it helps aid muscle recovery and makes sure I don't get the munchies at 11am. You can always make this the night before and pop it in a takeaway cup to bring to the gym.

Serves 1

350ml coconut milk
   or almond milk
½ avocado, peeled
   and stoned
2 Medjool dates, pitted
1 tbsp chia seeds
½ tsp vanilla extract
2 tbsp protein powder
   (I love hemp powder!)
large handful of kale,
   washed, chopped and
   stems removed

Place everything in a blender and process until smooth. Then drink straight away or keep in the fridge overnight.

Four Porridges

Porridge in PJs is my go-to winter look. I love curling up with a comforting bowl of goodness. The difficult bit is choosing which topping to go for! Here are four of my favourite winter toppings, all equally nutritious and delicious.

Poached Pear

V **DF** **15**

Serves 1

1 pear
1 tbsp maple syrup
2 cloves
1 tsp ground cinnamon
¼ tsp freshly grated nutmeg
50g rolled oats
300ml coconut milk or almond milk
1 tbsp coconut sugar

Peel, halve and core the pear and put the halves in a small pot, lying down on their sides. Cover in water and add the maple syrup, cloves, cinnamon and nutmeg. Bring to the boil, then reduce to a simmer with the lid on and cook for 20 minutes until softened.

Meanwhile, put the oats, milk and coconut sugar in another pot, stir well and cook for 5–7 minutes until the oats are soft and have absorbed most of the milk. Stir in 2 tablespoons of the pear poaching juices and top with the poached pear. Serve warm, but watch out for the cloves!

Cacao Nib and Almond Butter

V **DF** **PP** **15**

Serves 1

1 tbsp pecans
50g rolled oats
300ml coconut milk or almond milk
1 tbsp coconut sugar
1 tsp coconut oil
1 tbsp cacao nibs
1 tsp desiccated coconut
2 tbsp almond butter

Heat a small frying pan to a medium–high heat, then pop in the pecans and toast for 2–3 minutes. Remember to shake the pan to prevent them burning. Then tip out on to a plate on the side to cool.

Place the oats, milk and coconut sugar in a pot and cook for 3–4 minutes until the oats are soft and have absorbed most of the milk. Stir through the coconut oil. Top the porridge with the cacao nibs, desiccated coconut and toasted pecans, and drizzle over the almond butter.

Serves 1

50g rolled oats

300ml coconut milk
or almond milk

1 tbsp coconut sugar

20g good-quality
chocolate

1 clementine

2 tbsp toasted
hazelnuts, chopped

Clementine, Chocolate and Toasted Hazelnut

V S PP 15

Put the oats, milk and coconut sugar in a pot and cook for 3–4 minutes until the oats are soft and have absorbed most of the milk. Meanwhile, carefully melt the chocolate in a heatproof bowl over a pot of simmering water on a low heat.

Peel the clementine and slice across the middle into several rounds. Place on top of the porridge, then sprinkle on the hazelnuts and drizzle over the chocolate.

Serves 1

1 tbsp coconut oil or
butter

2 apples, cored and
thinly sliced

1 tsp ground cinnamon

2 tbsp coconut sugar,
plus extra to serve

50g rolled oats

300ml coconut milk
or almond milk

1 tbsp raisins

Apple Pie

V DF 15

Heat the oil in a pan, then add the apple slices, cinnamon and 1 tablespoon of the coconut sugar. Cook for 5–6 minutes until the apples turn golden brown.

While the apples are cooking, make the porridge. Place the oats, milk, raisins and the remaining tablespoon of coconut sugar in a pot and cook for 3–4 minutes until the oats are soft and have absorbed most of the milk.

Layer the porridge and apple mixtures on top of each other in a bowl or glass, sprinkle a little extra coconut sugar on top and serve.

Four Winter Side Dishes

Serves 4

100g kale, thinly sliced
1 tbsp honey
1 tbsp grainy mustard
pinch of salt
1 tbsp olive oil
25g toasted hazelnuts, chopped

Steamed Kale with Honey Mustard Dressing

V GF DF S 15

Kale is so nutritious. It's loaded with vitamins, minerals, fibre, antioxidants and various bioactive compounds. Kale contains vitamins C, A, K1 and B6, as well as potassium, calcium, magnesium, copper and manganese. I particularly like eating kale in the evening as the magnesium helps your muscles relax and you'll have an amazing night's sleep. Amazing sleep= glowing skin!

Steam the kale for 4–5 minutes over a pan of simmering water, then drain. Meanwhile, whisk the honey, mustard and salt together. Pour the olive oil over the cooked kale and toss to coat, then add the honey mustard dressing and mix through. Top with the hazelnuts.

Serves 4

500g parsnips, peeled
5 tbsp coconut oil or butter
salt and freshly ground black pepper, to taste

Crispy Parsnip Fries

V GF DF 30

Parsnips are a warming food. Yes, this dish is a comfort food too, but warming foods help to raise the energy of your organs, improve the circulation and dispel the cold. Get your digestive system fired up with this awesome root veg and serve with a side of steak!

Preheat the oven to 220°C/425°F/gas mark 7. Cut the parsnips into thin fries. Melt the coconut oil in a roasting tin, add the parsnip fries and toss in the oil with a good grind of salt and pepper. Roast in the oven until golden brown, taking them out to flip over halfway through the cooking time. The parsnips will cook in 15–20 minutes, depending on the size of your fries.

Clementine and Chicory Salad (V) GF DF 15

Serves 4

4 clementines
4 chicory heads
2 tbsp lemon juice
4 tbsp olive oil
big pinch of salt
100g pomegranate seeds

I love this fruity salad! Chicory is definitely an underrated veggie. It helps to ease digestive problems, prevent heartburn and detoxify the liver, and these are just some of its superpowers. It's awesomely crunchy and makes a great salad or crudité!

Peel the clementines and slice them into 1cm-thick rounds. Cut the bottom off each chicory and fan out the leaves on a plate. Top with the clementine rounds. Whisk the lemon juice with the olive oil and the salt, and pour over the salad. Top with the pomegranate seeds.

Roasted Celeriac Wedges (V) GF

Serves 4

1 celeriac
1 tsp ground cumin
½ tsp cayenne pepper
½ tsp smoked paprika
big pinch of salt
2 tbsp butter, melted

The poor celeriac is a bit ugly looking, and you may have to go searching in a bigger supermarket or farmers' market to find one. But don't judge a book by its cover, they're so awesome as chip-like wedges! As they're great source of dietary fibre, you'll have a happy tummy too – which means happy skin!

Preheat the oven to 200°C/400°F/gas mark 6. Peel and cut the celeriac into wedges. Mix the spices together with the salt. Brush the wedges with the melted butter and then rub in the spice mixture and place on a roasting tray. Roast for 45–50 minutes, turning over halfway through the cooking time, until golden and cooked through.

Butter Bean and Cauliflower Soup

(V) GF DF PP

I love a bowl of soup on a cold night. Cauliflower has a gorgeous warming taste and when it's blended with butter beans it goes super creamy. You'll feel full from the protein in the butter beans, while the chilli will leave you feeling warm and ready to take on the winter cold.

Serves 4

1 tbsp coconut oil
  or butter

1 white onion, finely
  chopped

salt and freshly ground
  black pepper, to taste

1 tbsp chopped fresh
  thyme leaves

4 garlic cloves, crushed

1 tsp dried chilli flakes

1 cauliflower, roughly
  chopped

400g can butter beans,
  rinsed and drained

400ml can coconut milk

500ml veggie or
  chicken stock

pinch of cayenne pepper

Place the oil in a large pot over a medium heat and sauté the onion with a big pinch of salt for 7 minutes until it turns golden. Add the thyme, garlic and chilli flakes and cook for 30 seconds. Then add the cauliflower and butter beans, stir them around in the spices and pour over the coconut milk and stock. Add another pinch of salt, bring to the boil, then turn down the heat and simmer for 30 minutes. Blend the soup until smooth, season with salt and pepper, then stir in the cayenne.

This goes very well with a toasted slice or two of the cashew loaf (see page 144).

Buckwheat and Kale Salad

(V) GF DF D 30

With Radishes, Pomegranate and Balsamic Dressing

I love this warm salad; it's super colourful and has so many different textures. Pomegranate gives any salad a wonderful pop of juiciness, and here will turn anyone on to a kale salad.

Serves 2

100g buckwheat
pinch of salt
200g kale, shredded
100g radishes, sliced
seeds from 1 pomegranate
25g pistachios

For the dressing

2 tbsp pomegranate seeds
2 tbsp balsamic vinegar
1 date, pitted
1 tsp grated orange zest
2 tbsp orange juice

Rinse the buckwheat then put in a pot with a pinch of salt. Add 250ml water and bring to the boil, then simmer for 12 minutes until the buckwheat is just cooked through and the liquid is absorbed. Meanwhile, steam the kale with another pinch of salt over a pan of simmering water for 8–10 minutes, then drain.

Put all the dressing ingredients in a food processor or blender and process until smooth. Heat in a small pan until the dressing reduces by half.

Place 1 tablespoon of the reduced dressing in a frying pan over a medium heat. Tip in the steamed kale, add another pinch of salt and sauté for a few minutes. Then throw in the cooked buckwheat and stir together. Serve topped with the radishes, pomegranate seeds and pistachios, and with the rest of the dressing drizzled over.

Two Winter Lunch Boxes

Smoked mackerel is the perfect lunch when you're on the go. Pair with beetroot for a Scandinavian-inspired lunchtime treat! On days when you don't fancy fish, just whip up this glorious sweet potato and coconut slaw to nourish your body with some much-needed goodness.

Smoked Mackerel and Beetroot Pot GF DF D PP 15

Serves 1

1 beetroot, peeled and grated

1 apple, grated

1 tbsp chopped fresh chives

1 tbsp olive oil

salt and freshly ground black pepper, to taste

1 smoked mackerel fillet, flaked

Mix the grated beetroot, apple, chives, oil and seasoning together and pop in your lunch box. Top with the flaked mackerel.

Sweet Potato with Coconut Slaw V GF DF S

Serves 1

1 large or 2 small sweet potatoes, cut into wedges

1 tbsp coconut oil or butter, melted

salt and freshly ground black pepper, to taste

1/8 white cabbage

1 carrot

1 tbsp olive oil

2 tbsp coconut yogurt or natural yogurt

1 spring onion

2 tbsp pumpkin seeds

Preheat the oven to 200°C/400°F/gas mark 6.

Spread out the sweet potato wedges in a roasting tray and pour over the coconut oil. Shake the wedges on the tray to make sure they are covered, then grind over plenty of salt and pepper. Roast in the oven for 45 minutes, until the sweet potatoes are golden and cooked through. Take out and leave on the side to cool.

While the wedges are cooling, thinly slice the cabbage and grate the carrot. Mix with the olive oil, yogurt and a pinch of salt. Slice the spring onion into fine slivers. Add to the cabbage slaw and mix again. Spoon the slaw into your lunch box and top with the sweet potato wedges. Throw over the pumpkin seeds to finish.

Two Winter Take-to-Work Snacks

Miso soup is such a simple and yummy dish to warm you up on a chilly afternoon. Have the ingredients at your desk so that you can simply boil the kettle and whip this up in a flash!

Serves 1

1 tbsp miso paste
pinch of dried
   chilli flakes
1 tsp dulse flakes
   (optional)

Miso Soup

(V) GF DF I5

Put the miso paste into a bowl or mug, pour over 200ml of boiling water and stir to dissolve. Add the chilli flakes and dulse, if using, and mix together. Serve warm.

Serves 6–8

4 large sweet potatoes
3 tbsp coconut oil
1 tbsp fennel seeds
2 tbsp coconut sugar
3 tbsp ground almonds
big pinch of salt
   and freshly ground
   black pepper
200g celery sticks,
   cut into batons
200g chicory heads,
   leaves separated

Sweet Potato Dip with Crudités

(V) GF DF S

Preheat the oven to 200°C/400°F/gas mark 6.

Cut the sweet potatoes into chip-like shapes and place on a large roasting tray. Melt the coconut oil and pour over the sweet potatoes, rubbing it in so the chips are evenly covered. Sprinkle over the fennel seeds, coconut sugar, ground almonds and a big pinch of salt and pepper. Toss the sweet potatoes using your hands so that everything is evenly distributed. Roast in the oven for 40 minutes until cooked through and golden on the outside.

Leave to cool, then blend the cooked sweet potato chips in a food processor to form a smooth dip. Serve with the celery and chicory as crudités.

Any leftover dip can be stored in the fridge for 4-5 days.

Basmati Rice Bowl
with Crispy Brussels

Ⓥ GF DF Ⓢ 15

Brussels sprouts are like Marmite – you either love them or hate them. I love them, and in winter I just can't get enough. They are full of vitamin K for blood and bone health, and vitamin C for radiant skin! Mixed with sweet cranberries, this is a seriously satisfying dinner dish!

Serves 2

100g basmati rice
salt, to taste
½ tsp lemon juice
20g dried cranberries
25g toasted pine nuts
25g pistachios
1 tbsp chopped fresh dill
1 tbsp chopped fresh
   parsley
1 tbsp chopped fresh mint

For the crispy Brussels

2 tbsp coconut oil
   or butter
200g Brussels sprouts
2 tbsp maple syrup
2 garlic cloves, crushed
pinch of salt

First, make the crispy Brussels. Heat the oil in a large pan over a medium–high heat. Add the Brussels to the pan, then the maple syrup, garlic and the salt. Stir and sauté for 15 minutes until the Brussels are golden and cooked through.

While this is cooking, prepare the rice. Rinse and place in a large pot with 185ml of water and a pinch of salt. Pop the lid on, bring to the boil, then add the lemon juice to the water and stir. Cover the pan again, lower the heat and leave to simmer for 8 minutes. The rice should be cooked through and the liquid absorbed. Take off the heat and fluff with a fork.

To serve, mix together the cooked rice, crispy Brussels, dried cranberries, nuts, herbs and a pinch of salt.

Chicken Breast

GF DF PP 30

with Spiced Carrots and Cauliflower Tabbouleh

I love North African spices, especially when mixed with sweet carrots. So this dish is inspired by Morocco! Cumin and ginger warm the body, while the turmeric is great for skin because of its incredible anti-inflammatory properties. These golden super spices save the day in the kitchen and are great for your skin!

Serves 2

2 garlic cloves, crushed
½ tsp ground cumin
½ tsp ground coriander
salt, to taste
2 chicken breasts
1 tbsp coconut oil
1 tsp freshly grated ginger
¼ tsp turmeric
2 large carrots, cut into
  1cm chunks
1 small cauliflower, leaves
  and core removed
1 large beef tomato,
  chopped into cubes
2 tsp toasted sesame seeds
seeds from 1 pomegranate,
  or 200g seeds
1 tbsp olive oil
2 tbsp finely chopped
  fresh parsley

Mix together the garlic, cumin, coriander and a big pinch of salt. Rub on to the chicken breasts and leave to marinate overnight if possible.

Heat half the coconut oil in a large pan and add the ginger and turmeric. Stir, then add the carrots and sauté for a few minutes. Add the rest of the oil and the chicken, then pan-fry the chicken for 6 minutes on each side until cooked through. Keep stirring the carrots around, adding a tablespoon of water every few minutes so they don't burn. Remove from the heat when the chicken is ready.

Grate the cauliflower into small pieces or process it in a food processor until it forms into rice-like grains. Steam for 3 minutes over a pan of simmering water, then drain. Mix with the tomato, sesame seeds, pomegranate seeds, olive oil and a pinch of salt to make the tabbouleh.

Plate up the tabbouleh with the chicken and carrots on top, and scatter over the parsley. Serve warm.

Indian Spiced Vegetable Curry

V GF S 30

Curries by nature are very warming as they contain lots of spices that get your body feeling the heat. Kieran is half Indian and makes an amazing curry, so I always take inspiration from him when putting spices together. I use sweet potatoes in this dish because they're at their best in the winter, they give us energy and they're filling!

Serves 2–3

1 tbsp coconut oil
   or butter
2 white onions, chopped
1 dried red chilli, chopped
2 cardamom pods
1 tsp ground cinnamon
2 garlic cloves, crushed
2 parsnips, chopped
   into chunks
salt, to taste and freshly
   ground black pepper
2 sweet potatoes, chopped
   into chunks
400ml can coconut milk
3 tbsp ground almonds
100g frozen peas
1 tbsp lemon juice
1 tbsp finely chopped
   fresh coriander

For the yogurt dressing

1 tbsp freshly grated ginger
1 garlic clove, crushed
150g Greek yogurt
½ tsp turmeric
big pinch of salt
pinch of freshly ground
   black pepper

Heat the oil in a large pan and add the onions. Sauté for 5 minutes, then add the chilli, cardamom pods, cinnamon and garlic. Stir for 30 seconds to release the spice flavours, then add the sweet potatoes and parsnips and a big pinch of salt. Stir again for 30 seconds to coat the potatoes. Pour in the coconut milk and add the ground almonds, then lower the heat and simmer for 30 minutes.

Meanwhile, whisk the yogurt dressing ingredients together.

Just before you're ready to serve, throw the frozen peas into the curry and stir. Add the lemon juice and chopped coriander and season with a little more salt and a pinch of pepper to taste. Serve warm with a dollop of the yogurt dressing on top.

Any leftover yogurt dressing can be stored in an airtight container in the fridge for 3 days.

Oregano and Thyme Spiced Beef Stew GF PP

When you think of beef you don't often think of glowing skin, but beef is actually a nutritional powerhouse. Grass-fed beef contains CLA, which has anti-ageing benefits and also contains omega 3 fatty acids, vitamin E and energy-boosting B vitamins. This stew is so comforting and everything you need on a chilly day. Rich in spices and flavour, it's the perfect meal for the family to enjoy. Make it in advance as this dish ages well.

Serves 4

salt and freshly ground
   black pepper, to taste
500g stewing beef, cut into
   1 inch chunks
2 tbsp butter
2 white onions, finely
   chopped
3 garlic cloves, crushed
4 tbsp tomato concentrate
1 tbsp chopped fresh
   oregano leaves
1 tbsp chopped fresh
   thyme leaves
500ml beef stock
2 tbsp chopped fresh
   parsley

Grind plenty of salt and pepper over the beef. Heat half the butter in a large pot over a medium–high heat and add the meat. Cook for 2–3 minutes until brown, then remove to a plate on one side.

Turn down the heat to medium, put the onions and the rest of the butter into the pot, add a pinch of salt and cook for 7 minutes until golden. Add the garlic and cook for another minute. Throw the browned beef back in and add the tomato concentrate, oregano, thyme and a pinch of salt and pepper. Stir well for 30 seconds, then pour over the stock.

Pop the lid on, turn down the heat and simmer for 50 minutes until the meat has softened completely. Sprinkle over the parsley to serve.

Serve with sweet potato mash and salad.

Red Rice and Roasted Leeks Chimichurri Bowl

(V) GF DF (S) 30

In my opinion, red rice is so underrated. I love whipping up a red rice bowl for a good girly lunch, or a warming dinner for a night in at home with my boyfriend. Rice has a bad rep for having no flavour, so I've ramped it up with a herby, skin-glowing chimichurri. Leeks are naturally warming and have an amazing flavour when cooked.

Serves 2

100g red rice
salt, to taste
2 tbsp coconut oil
  or butter
4 leeks, chopped into
  1cm rings
2 garlic cloves, crushed
50g rocket
1 beef tomato, diced
25g pumpkin seeds

For the Chimichurri sauce

25g fresh flat-leaf parsley
10g fresh oregano
3 spring onions
3 garlic cloves
½ tsp crushed red
  pepper flakes
100ml olive oil
25ml red wine vinegar
3 tbsp fresh lemon juice
salt, to taste

Cook the red rice as per the packet instructions with a pinch of salt. Meanwhile, heat the coconut oil in a large frying pan. Add the leeks, garlic and a big pinch of salt, and sauté for 20 minutes until the leeks are golden brown and cooked through.

To make the chimichurri sauce, finely chop or mince the parsley and oregano, the spring onions and garlic. Put in a medium bowl and whisk in the red pepper flakes, olive oil, vinegar and lemon juice. Season with salt and mix thoroughly again.

To serve, put the cooked leeks, rocket and diced tomato in a bowl and toss together. Sprinkle over the pumpkin seeds and drizzle with 3 tablespoons of the chimichurri dressing.

You can keep the leftover dressing for 3–4 days in the fridge. It is fantastic for dressing salads.

Quinoa and Maple-Roasted Squash Bowl

If you're looking for a protein-rich veggie dish, you've turned to the right page. Squash season is awesome, and in winter that sweet squash hits the spot for a satisfying dinner. If you find yourself feeling cold, squash gives your organs energy, improves your circulation and will warm you right up. That means toasty fingertips and gorgeous rosy cheeks!

Serves 4

1 large butternut squash
4 shallots
2 tbsp coconut oil
   or butter, melted
2 tbsp maple syrup
salt, to taste
200g quinoa
200g purple sprouting
   broccoli
2 tbsp olive oil
1 tsp dried chilli flakes

Preheat the oven to 200°C/400°F/gas mark 6.

Peel the squash and chop it into 2½cm chunks. Cut the shallots into halves and remove their skin. Place the veggies in a roasting tray and drizzle over the coconut oil and maple syrup. Mix and rub into the squash and shallots, and sprinkle over a pinch of salt. Roast in the oven for 45–50 minutes until golden and cooked through.

While the veggies are in the oven, rinse the quinoa and place in a pot with 550ml of water and a pinch of salt. Bring to the boil, then turn down the heat and simmer for 15 minutes until the water is absorbed and the quinoa has softened. Steam the purple sprouting broccoli over a pot of simmering water for 3 minutes until almost cooked through, then drain.

Mix everything together on a platter with a pinch of salt. Drizzle over the olive oil and sprinkle on the chilli flakes. Serve warm.

Cashew and Chickpea Chicken Curry GF DF PP 30

Chickpeas are awesome, and teamed with cashew nuts and chicken, this curry hits the spot for a satisfying dinner. This is another great warming meal that's perfect for cold winter nights – the spiciness of the ginger and chilli will keep you toasty when the temperature drops!

Serves 2

1 tbsp coconut oil
   or butter
300g chicken thighs,
   chopped into strips
1 garlic clove, crushed
1 tsp freshly grated ginger
1 tbsp red Thai curry paste
1 tsp curry powder
400ml can coconut milk
1 tbsp tamari
3 tbsp almond butter,
   peanut butter or cashew
   nut butter
400g can chickpeas, rinsed
   and drained
25g cashews
2 tbsp chopped fresh
   coriander
juice of 1 lime

Heat the oil in a casserole or large pan. Add the chicken pieces and cook for 2–3 minutes until browned. Then add the garlic, ginger, curry paste and curry powder, and stir for 30 seconds to release the flavours.

Pour in the coconut milk and add the tamari, nut butter, chickpeas and cashews. Place the lid on, turn down the heat and simmer for 15 minutes until the chicken is cooked through.

Serve with the coriander and lime juice sprinkled over.

Spicy Bean Stew

V GF DF PP

In winter we crave soups and stews. While I do love a soup, sometimes I need something that feels more filling. There's nothing more comforting than the texture of sweet potatoes and kidney beans with gorgeous Middle Eastern spices. Kidney beans are nutrient packed and soak up the flavour of whatever they're simmering in!

Serves 6

3 carrots

2 yellow peppers, deseeded

2 sweet potatoes

2 tbsp coconut oil

1 large white onion, chopped

2 tsp ground cumin

2 tsp smoked paprika

1 red chilli, deseeded and finely chopped

1 tsp dried oregano

2 garlic cloves, crushed

2 x 400g cans chopped tomatoes

2 x 400g cans kidney beans, rinsed and drained

250ml vegetable stock

2 tbsp chopped fresh coriander, to serve

Chop the carrots, peppers and sweet potatoes into bite-sized cubes. Heat the coconut oil in a large pot, then throw in the onion, cumin, smoked paprika, chilli, oregano and a pinch of salt.

Cook for 6 minutes until the onion has browned, adding a little water if it gets too dry. Add the carrots, peppers and sweet potatoes. Pour over the tomatoes, beans and stock, and add another pinch of salt.

Turn down the heat and simmer for 1 hour with the lid on. Top with fresh coriander to serve.

My Favourite Dhal Recipe

V GF PP 30

Lentil dhal reminds me of one of my friends, Anjli, who always brings me a fresh batch made by her grandma. Lentils are an awesome source of veggie protein, and you can even have this as a side dish to a curry for a pick 'n' mix curry night. Quick to make and even easier to eat! Plus you can freeze this for a later date.

Serves 3–4

200g dried red lentils
salt, to taste
1 tbsp butter or ghee
1 onion, finely chopped
2 garlic cloves, crushed
2 tsp freshly grated ginger
200g chard leaves, sliced
1 tsp ground cumin
1 beef tomato, chopped
1 green chilli, finely
   chopped
1 bay leaf
1 tsp garam masala

Rinse the lentils, then place in a large saucepan, cover with 800ml of water and add 1 teaspoon of salt. Bring to the boil, then reduce to a simmer and cook for 10 minutes. Take off the heat.

While the lentils are cooking, heat the butter in a pan. Add the onion, garlic and ginger and cook for 5 minutes, then add the chard leaves, cumin, tomato, chilli and bay leaf, and cook for a further 5 minutes until the chard has wilted. Use a wooden spoon to crush the tomato down into a paste.

Once the tomatoey spice mix is ready, add the cooked lentils to the pan and stir everything together. Add the garam masala and a pinch of salt, if needed, then serve.

Slow-Roast Lamb Shoulder

GF S PP

with Celeriac Mash and Greens

Slow-roast lamb would be my last meal. I absolutely love how the meat falls off the bone. Because I find myself making it so often in the winter, I like to think of ways to mix it up. Celeriac mash is an exciting alternative to potatoes because it's got a unique celery-nutty flavour. The Swiss chard is brilliant for blood sugar regulation, as well as digestion, so it helps with dips of energy – especially post-eating!

Serves 6

2kg lamb shoulder, bone in

6 garlic cloves, crushed

2 sprigs of fresh thyme, leaves picked and chopped

2 sprigs of fresh rosemary, leaves picked and chopped

1 tsp salt

For the celeriac mash

2 celeriac, peeled and roughly chopped

1 tsp grainy mustard

1 tbsp butter

½ tsp salt

For the greens

2 bunches of Swiss chard

1 tbsp olive oil

1 tbsp chopped fresh parsley

pinch of salt

Preheat the oven to 200°C/400°F/gas mark 6.

Take the lamb shoulder and rub the garlic, thyme, rosemary and salt into the meat all over. Place in a casserole pot with the lid on, and put in the oven. Turn the oven down to 150°C/300°F/gas mark 2 and cook for 4 hours until the meat falls apart.

Shortly before the lamb is cooked, prepare the side dishes. Steam the celeriac over a pan of simmering water for 10 minutes until cooked through, then drain and place in a blender with the mustard, butter and salt. Steam the Swiss chard for 5–6 minutes, then drain and tip into a pan. Add the olive oil, parsley and salt. Sauté for a minute or two.

Serve the lamb with a dollop of mash and a serving of greens.

Pan-Fried Steak

GF DF PP 15

with Sweet Potato Mash, Toasted Mustard Seeds and Shallot Sauce

This is my favourite post-gym dinner. It's really quick to whip up and super comforting thanks to the mustard seed and shallot sauce. Shallots really help smooth the texture of your skin because they contain antioxidant flavanols.

Serves 2

2 rib-eye steaks (approx. 200g each)

salt and freshly ground black pepper, to taste

1 tsp mustard seeds

1 large sweet potato, cut into 2½cm chunks

1 tbsp avocado oil or butter

For the shallot sauce

1 tbsp avocado oil or butter

2 shallots, finely chopped

1 garlic clove, crushed

1 sprig of fresh rosemary, leaves picked and finely chopped

2 tbsp balsamic vinegar

200ml beef stock

Bring the steaks to room temperature and season with salt and pepper. Heat a small frying pan to a medium–high heat. Toast the mustard seeds for a minute, shaking the pan to prevent them burning, then tip on to a plate to cool.

Steam the sweet potato over a pan of simmering water for 10 minutes until soft, then drain and mash or blend until smooth with a big pinch of salt.

While the sweet potatoes are cooking, make the sauce. Heat the oil in a pan and add the shallots. Sauté for 4 minutes, then add the garlic, stir and cook for another minute. Add the rosemary, balsamic and beef stock to the pan. Reduce the heat and leave to simmer until the sauce reduces by half.

When everything else is ready, heat a griddle pan or frying pan to a high heat, add the oil and fry the seasoned steaks for 2 minutes on each side (or to your liking). Serve the steak with the mash, sprinkle over the mustard seeds and drizzle the shallot dressing over the top.

Raw Peanut Butter Bars

V GF DF S PP

I could easily sit and eat a whole tub of peanut butter with a spoon, so in an attempt to be more restrained I created these gorgeous bars. Warning: they're totally moreish but definitely more sophisticated than a messy tub. Plus peanut butter is a great source of vitamin E and protein, so this a perfect snack if your skin needs a boost or you work out a lot. If you prefer, swap for a different nut butter and mix it up!

Makes 8-10

For the crust

75g toasted hazelnuts, ground
2 tbsp raw cacao powder
2 tbsp maple syrup
1 tbsp coconut oil
pinch of salt

For the peanut butter filling

120g peanut butter
3 tbsp maple syrup
1 tbsp coconut oil, melted
pinch of salt

For the chocolate topping

30g cocoa powder
3 tbsp coconut oil, melted
3 tbsp maple syrup

Line a small roasting tray with baking paper. Place the crust ingredients in a bowl and mix together until fully combined. Press this into the lined tray and pop in the freezer while you make the filling.

Clean out the bowl and place the peanut butter filling ingredients in it. Mix well, then pour over the crust layer and pop in the freezer.

Combine the chocolate topping ingredients together, whisking well to break up any clumps. Continue whisking until it has the consistency of chocolate sauce, then pour it over the peanut butter layer and place back in the freezer.

After 30 minutes the bars should be firm. Using a sharp knife, cut into squares and keep in the fridge until ready to eat.

These will last for 2 weeks in the fridge, but will probably be eaten in 24 hours!

Easy-Peasy Coconut Cookies

V DF 15

Coconut cookies are a winter essential for me. They make me look forward to the summer as they've got a gorgeous sweet taste that reminds me of sunnier climates. These are crunchy and delicious – perfect for a movie night!

Makes 14 cookies

120g rolled oats
120g spelt flour
160g coconut sugar
½ tsp bicarbonate of soda
½ tsp salt
150g coconut oil, melted
1 large egg
2 tsp vanilla extract
50g coconut flakes or
    desiccated coconut

Preheat the oven to 180°C/350°F/gas mark 4 and line a baking tray with baking paper.

In a large bowl mix everything together apart from the coconut flakes to form a dough. Then stir through the coconut flakes. Using your hands, grab about a tablespoon of dough and roll into a ball, then place the ball on the paper-lined baking tray. Repeat with the rest of the mixture, placing the balls at least 10cm apart.

Bake for 10 minutes in the preheated oven until they have turned into golden-coloured cookies. Leave to cool on a wire rack, then dig in.

Lemon Drizzle Cake

V DF

This is my go-to birthday cake. I truly believe that you can follow a healthy diet and still have your favourite sweet treats . . . which is where the classic lemon drizzle cake comes in. A gorgeous soft cake with a sharp lemon drizzle, this is the perfect teatime treat.

Serves 12

300g coconut sugar
130g coconut oil or butter, plus extra for greasing
175g spelt flour
½ tsp baking powder
½ tsp bicarbonate of soda
¼ tsp salt
250g coconut yogurt or Greek yogurt
2 large eggs
grated zest and juice of 1 lemon
1 tsp vanilla extract
desiccated coconut, to serve

For the drizzle

1 tbsp lemon juice
1 tbsp maple syrup

Preheat the oven to 170°C/325°F/gas mark 3 and grease a 20cm cake tin.

Cream the sugar and oil in a food processor. Sift the flour, baking powder, bicarb and salt into a large mixing bowl. In another bowl, whisk the yogurt and eggs together and stir into the creamed sugar mixture.

Then pour this wet mixture into the dry ingredients. Add the lemon zest, 2 tablespoons of the juice and the vanilla. Mix gently, then pour into the greased cake tin. Bake in the oven for 50 minutes to 1 hour until the cake is cooked through so that a knife comes out clean.

Remove the cake from the oven and allow to cool on a wire rack. Warm the drizzle ingredients in a pot, stirring to mix, then after 3–4 minutes, pour over the cake. Finish by sprinkling over a little desiccated coconut.

Meal Plans

Spring

	Breakfast	Lunch	Snack	Dinner
Monday	Glowing Breakfast Muffins (page 20)	Roasted Cauliflower with Romesco, Capers and Toasted Hazelnuts (page 36)	Rice Crispy Squares (page 50)	Greek Goodness Salad (page 44)
Tuesday	Chocolate Protein Powered Smoothie (page 28)	Buckwheat Tabbouleh with Rocket, Radishes and Spring Onion (page 48)	Roasted Chickpeas (page 50)	Beef Kebabs with Mint Raita (page 54)
Wednesday	Glowing Breakfast Muffins (page 20)	Beef Kebabs with Mint Raita (page 54)	Rice Crispy Squares (page 50)	Maple and Miso Red Rice Salad (page 64)
Thursday	Chargrilled Asparagus and Chimichurri on Toast (page 25)	Maple and Miso Red Rice salad (page 64)	Roasted Chickpeas (page 50)	Tray-Baked Chicken with Tomato and Fennel (page 59)
Friday	Avocado with Maple Miso Dressing and Pomegranate on Toast (page 24)	Tray-Baked Chicken with Tomato and Fennel (page 59)	Rhubarb and Coconut Rice Pudding (page 68)	Lamb Chops with Parsnip Mash and Asparagus (page 66)
Saturday	Zesty Ricotta Pancakes (page 31)	Prawn, Grapefruit and Avocado Salad (page 48)	Coffee Pecan Muffin (page 74)	Grilled Herb-Crusted Mackerel (page 56)
Sunday	Lemon and Pea Pesto Smash on Toast (page 24)	Fish Skewers with Parsnip Chips (page 62)	Rice Crispy Squares (page 50)	Spanish Chickpea Stew with Chorizo and Spinach (page 60)

Summer

	Breakfast	Lunch	Snack	Dinner
Monday	Raspberry and Chia Overnight Oats (page 82)	Summer Lovin' Bowl (page 106)	Tamari-Roasted Pumpkin Seeds (page 113)	Steak Fajitas with Roasted Peppers and Corn (page 114)
Tuesday	Berry Nice Zoats (page 83)	Steak Fajitas with Roasted Peppers and Corn (page 114)	Cannellini Dip with Crudités (page 113)	Thai Green Chicken Curry (page 118)
Wednesday	Green Shakshuka (page 88)	Thai Green Chicken Curry (page 118)	Tamari-Roasted Pumpkin Seeds (page 113)	Pistachio-Crusted Sea Bass with Shaved Fennel and Courgetti (page 124)
Thursday	Strawberry Basil Smoothie (page 90)	Pistachio-Crusted Sea Bass with Shaved Fennel and Courgetti (page 124)	Cannellini Dip with Crudités (page 113)	Roasted Cod with Charred Courgettes and Peppers (page 120)
Friday	Chilli Scrambled Eggs with Mushrooms on Toast (page 93)	Asparagus, Boiled Egg, Olive and Green Bean Bowl (page 110)	Almond and Blueberry Tart slice (page 130)	Middle Eastern Mezze Bowl (page 101)
Saturday	Sweetcorn Fritters with Tomato Salsa and Avocado (page 80)	Potato, Pea, Radish, Brown Rice and Rocket Salad (page 124)	2 Madeleines (page 128)	Whole Spiced Chicken with Baby Cos and Carrots (page 123)
Sunday	Vegan Banana and Peanut Butter Loaf (page 87)	Asian Spiced Mixed Grain Bowl (page 102)	Raw Chocolate Peanut Butter Brownie Bites (page 135)	Charred Corn and Tomato Pesto Pasta (page 117)

Autumn

	Breakfast	Lunch	Snack	Dinner
Monday	Black Rice Porridge with Berries and Caramelised Banana (page 140)	Carrot, Pea and Coconut Curry (page 177)	Four-Ingredient Granola Bar (page 168)	Torn Chicken salad (page 160)
Tuesday	Three-Ingredient Banana Pancakes (page 142)	Torn Chicken Salad (page 160)	Peanut Butter Toffee Popcorn (page 168)	Roasted Beetroot and Lentil Salad (page 164)
Wednesday	Avocado and Halloumi with Toasted Sesame Seeds on Toast (page 146)	Roasted Beetroot and Lentil Salad (page 164)	Four-Ingredient Granola Bar (page 168)	Baked Sea Bream and Lentil Parcels with Green Goddess Pesto (page 178)
Thursday	Lean and Green Courgette Omelette (page 151)	Baked Sea Bream and Lentil Parcels with Green Goddess Pesto (page 178)	Four-Ingredient Granola Bar (page 168)	Cumin Roasted Aubergine stuffed with Quinoa Tabbouleh (page 182)
Friday	Fig and Goat's Cheese on Toast (page 147)	Cumin Roasted Aubergine Stuffed with Quinoa Tabbouleh (page 182)	Peanut Butter Toffee Popcorn (page 168)	Squash and Tomato Coconut Curry (page 189)
Saturday	Cashew Loaf with Avocado (page 144)	Middle Eastern Quinoa Chicken Pot (page 167)	Plum and Almond Cake slice (page 198)	Chicken Ramen (page 180)
Sunday	Cashew Loaf with Scrambled Eggs (page 144)	Buckwheat Noodle Salad with Broccoli and Pak Choi (page 167)	Mini Crumble (page 195)	Sweet Potato and Broccoli Cakes (page 174)

Winter

	Breakfast	Lunch	Snack	Dinner
Monday	Wilted Spinach, Feta and Dukkah Omelette (page 209)	Immunity-Proof Chicken and Ginger Soup (page 223)	Sweet Potato Dip with Crudités (page 231)	Indian Spiced Vegetable Curry (page 236)
Tuesday	Gym Bunny Smoothie (page 210)	Indian Spiced Vegetable Curry (page 236)	Miso Soup (page 231)	Red Rice and Roasted Leeks Chimichurri Bowl (page 240)
Wednesday	Poached Pear Porridge (page 212)	Red Rice and Roasted Leeks Chimichurri Bowl (page 240)	Sweet Potato Dip with Crudités (page 231)	Cashew and Chickpea Chicken Curry (page 245)
Thursday	Cacao Nib and Almond Butter Porridge (page 212)	Cashew and Chickpea Chicken Curry (page 245)	Miso Soup (page 231)	Spicy Bean Stew (page 247)
Friday	Apple Pie Porridge (page 213)	Spicy Bean Stew (page 247)	Sweet Potato Dip with Crudités (page 231)	Pan-Fried Steak with Sweet Potato Mash and Shallot Sauce (page 252)
Saturday	Quinoa Pancakes with Blood Orange Slices (page 206)	Smoked Mackeral and Beetroot Pot (page 228)	Lemon Drizzle Cake slice (page 258)	Slow-Roast Lamb Shoulder with Celeriac Mash and Greens (page 251)
Sunday	Clementine, Chocolate and Toasted Hazelnut Porridge (page 213)	Sweet Potato with Coconut Slaw (page 228)	Raw Peanut Butter Bar (page 254)	My Favourite Dhal Recipe (page 248)

Index

Acknowledgements

Firstly, I'd like to thank my amazing publishers at Orion – thank you for saying yes to my first book three years ago! I'd also like to thank my wonderful editor, Anna, who is incredibly smart, creative and always a joy to be around. A massive thank you to my manager Alice and her team for always believing in me and for helping me to grow. To my gorgeous boyfriend Kieran, who I love with all my heart – thanks for being there to test all the recipes!

Thank you to Anna, Jen, Lucy and Ben for being Team Glow! To everyone who worked on the photo shoot for this book, thanks for all your help making the food look so delicious and for making me glow! Finally, thank you to you for buying this book! I hope you love it as much as I do. Now let's get glowing!

For more delicious recipes, features, videos and exclusives from Orion's cookery writers, and to sign up for our 'Recipe of the Week' email visit bybookorbycook.co.uk

Follow us

 @bybookorcook @bybookorbycook

Find us

 facebook.com/bybookorbycook

First published in Great Britain in 2017 by Trapeze, an imprint of The Orion Publishing Group Ltd Carmelite House, 50 Victoria Embankment, London EC4Y 0DZ

An Hachette UK company

10 9 8 7 6 5 4 3 2 1
Copyright © Madeleine Shaw 2017

The moral right of Madeleine Shaw to be identified as the author of this work has been asserted in accordance with the Copyright, Designs and Patents Act of 1988.

A CIP catalogue record for this book is available from the British Library.

Every effort has been made to ensure that the information in the book is accurate. The information in this book may not be applicable in each individual case so it is advised that professional medical advice is obtained for specific health matters and before changing any medication or dosage. Neither the publisher nor author accepts any legal responsibility for any personal injury or other damage or loss arising from the use of the information in this book. In addition if you are concerned about your diet or exercise regime and wish to change them, you should consult a health practitioner first.

ISBN: 978 1 409 17047 1

Lifestyle photography: Emma Gutteridge
Food photography: Martin Poole
Design: Abi Hartshorne
Food styling: Bianca Nice, Rob Morris
Prop styling: Kimberly Espinel

Printed in Italy

MIX
Paper from responsible sources
FSC® C023419

www.orionbooks.co.uk